THE STEP-BY-STEP BOOK OF
DRIED BOUQUETS

by Roberta Moffitt

Completely Revised 2nd Edition

Library of Congress Catalog Card Number
75-20781

Companion Book:
THE STEP-BY-STEP BOOK OF
PRESERVED FLOWERS
by Roberta Moffitt
$3.95 Ppd.

Published by
Roberta Moffitt Designs, P.O. Box 3597, Wilmington, DE 19807

A Fall Basket of Everlastings, See variation p. 5

The Color Pages

A Night in Vienna with Williamsburg China, see p. 61

3

Country French Flowers, see p. 80

Centerpiece with Plate, see p. 64

The Dolphin Candlesticks, see p. 107

Williamsburg Delft Jar, see page 84

Peonies and Pussywillows, p. 114

Gift From Your Garden, see p. 104

The Williamsburg Bricks, see p. 88

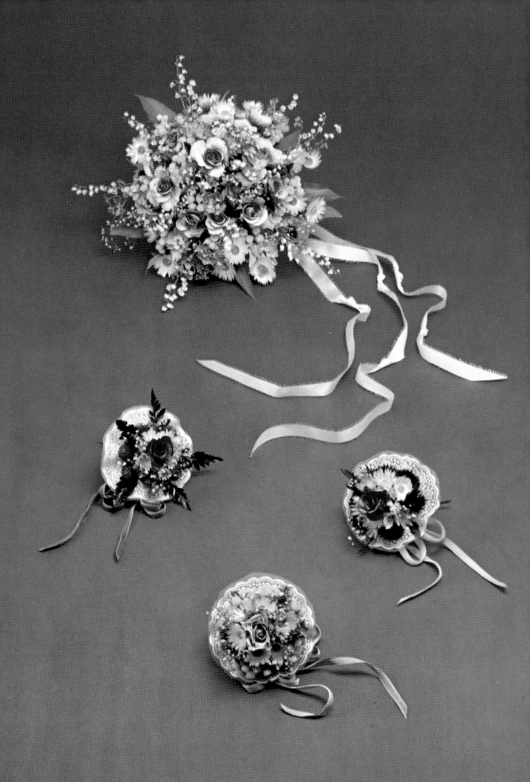

A Bride's Bouquet in Antique Smoke Bell, see page 120
Nosegays, see page 118

12

A Wedding Memory in Shadowbox, see page 125
Flowers Under a Dome, see page 122

Below: Williamsburg Five Finger Posey Holder, see page 92

Small Delft Centerpiece, see page 69; a Spring Basket, see page 55; Small Round Centerpiece [in tin], see page 48; A Pewter Salt Shaker, see page 129; A Demi-Tasse Cup, see page 131

Pair of Bells or Baskets, see p. 67

Seeing Double—A Small Pair, see p. 133

16

A Pastel Centerpiece, p. 51

A Centerpiece of Yellows, p. 58

Redware Pot of Everlastings, see page 75

The Country French Figurine: see page 99

*A Branch and Peony
—The Modern Look,
see page 102*

Springtime'' Natural Wood Sculpture, see p. 111

*Flowers in
Antique Lamp, see
A Variation, p. 98*

Antique Glass Vase, see p. 96

The Decorative Large Bouquet, see p. 78

Contents

Contents continued

Contents continued

Introduction

Dried flower arranging is one of the more important of the decorative arts. Today, with the high cost of fresh flowers, this early American art using natural dried flowers in decorative bouquets has become more important than ever before.

Lasting, colorful bouquets of dried flowers were a hallmark of 18th century American living, and are equally important to 20th century life styles. Traditionally, dried flower arrangements were associated with autumn, but the convenience and beauty of natural looking preserved flowers has become a fall, winter and spring decoration.

The step-by-step method, or "show and tell" with sequence pictures, has accounted for the tremendous success of my first book, *"The Step-by-Step Book of PRESERVED FLOWERS"*. For many years, I taught groups of women to arrange dried flowers and found that most of them had difficulty learning to wire and tape the flowers. When they mastered this technique, they had difficulty in the placement of various types and sizes of flowers and leaves. I remembered when I was associated with Good Housekeeping Magazine, we adopted a mythical teenager named "Susan" and wrote all of our recipes in the step-by-step technique so she would find them easy to follow. When a recipe was ready for publication, the question was, "Could Susan do it?".

These flower arrangements are written for all the Susans, whether 16 or 60, who want to make colorful dried flower arrangements for home and gifts. In the following pages, I have tried to lead the arranger through the steps of selecting and preparing the container, then building a background of leaves and filler materials to disguise the mechanics so the finished result will look as though it had been freshly picked. A simple, easy formula to determine height, width and depth is also included. Since it is seldom possible to have all the flowers called for in any given arrangement, there are alternate flower and color selections from which to choose.

Flower arrangements are grouped together in four sections, making selection easier. Those arrangements specifically listed as centerpieces could also be used for coffee tables and for other areas in the home. Some of the large, one-sided arrangements would be appropriate for use in flower shows. I have tried to use variety and imagination in the selection of flowers and colors to introduce the reader to the unlimited beauty that is there, available for your use. A special chapter suggests ways to use the flowers from a bride's bouquet for a permanent keepsake.

Decorating with flowers

When you are ready to put it all together, make a list of the bouquets you want to make for each room in your home. Look over your collection of containers to see which are most appropriate in size and color for specific use. You may need containers for one-sided bouquets for the hall table and perhaps for a mantel. Small, attractive simple containers for little in-the-round bouquets for bedrooms, and some plain round or oval containers for dining centerpieces.

Consider the colors and furnishings in each room and the degree of formality which will determine whether to use silver, pewter or brass, or porcelain, crystal or pottery. Consider, too, the paintings in the rooms, the drapery fabric or wall coverings and tie in these colors with your flower arrangements. Avoid over-matching, however, since the exact colors frequently found in fabrics are sometimes better enhanced by a mixture of pastel flower colors or light to dark shades of a single color.

A variation of round and spike forms makes a bouquet natural looking and avoids the monotony of all one flower type. At the same time, don't select so many different flowers they become confusing to arrange; it is easier and the result will be more pleasing if you use just a few types of flowers. If you are a determined realist, you may choose to group together only those flowers that bloom simultaneously in spring, summer or fall. I think it is more fun to mix the seasons in the manner of the early Flemish artists who painted flower arrangements using tulips with roses, daffodils, lilies and ladybugs!

Most of the photographs in this book show Line-Mass Arrangements. A mass arrangement does not mean packing a lot of flowers into a container. All good mass arrangements begin with a plan—usually a triangle. The sketches illustrating *Guide Posts and Guide Lines,* p. 33, are basic lines for use in mass arrangements and are used for all the arrangements in the color photographs in this book, except for the *Modern Branch with Peony* on p. 102.

Modern arrangements are more stark, use few flowers and frequently incorporate beautifully hand-crafted ceramic containers or very informal ones, making each arrangement a separate experience. It would be very difficult to duplicate most modern arrangements unless you have exactly the same container, as the container is an important part of the over-all design. This is true also of the modern school of Japanese arranging. Large, single flowers, beautifully preserved with a few perfect leaves, have unlimited possibilities for use in modern and Japanese arrangements.

Guide posts and guide lines

For Beginners

Take plenty of time: The selection of flowers, glueing, taping and spraying requires time and patience. Once these are finished, the bouquet will go together quickly. I have never found any shortcuts: if you omit glueing and spraying, you also shorten the life of your bouquet.

A bouquet frequently requires two or three hours to put together from start to finish. It may help to put it together in three stages: prepare the container and cover Oasis with German statice. Select and prepare the flowers, stemming, glueing and spraying. Then put it all together on another day.

The main axis: Each dried arrangement has a main axis or root point from which emerge as many stems as possible, just as the stems in a plant emerge from one point. Visualize the trunk of a tree. The trunk rises from the base with limbs radiating in a natural spiral: the longest and largest limbs are low and the shorter more delicate limbs radiate close to the top. No two limbs are exactly the same size nor exactly opposite each other—they are asymmetrical. (See sketch p. 33).

When stems radiate from the Main Axis, they are anchored at the center and extend out gracefully. An arrangement made by this method has stems close together in a small area in the center with some flowers looking directly upward, some looking to the right or left, and a few cascading outward over the base of the container.

Place the tallest and smallest flowers vertically at top center, gradually radiating downward with increasingly larger flowers on a gentle S curve or spiral from right to left, down to and below the base of the container (see Spiral and Zigzag sketches p. 33). Some flowers should be placed deeper in the bouquet for contrast and avoidance of a pincushion appearance. Study the color photographs and notice how this zigzagging shows in each one.

No pincushions! Some dried arrangements resemble a pincushion with flowers all placed at one level forming an unbroken, monotonous mound. The stems in the bouquet are placed like porcupine quills, with no discernible main axis. If you want a natural looking bouquet, avoid this.

Don't cross stems: Some stems at the main axis may be in view when the bouquet is completed. They should look natural and should not cross over each other and stand apart from those in the center. If this should happen (and it sometimes does), reach in carefully with pliers, loosen stem and place it closer to the center. See sketches at right.

YES   **NO**

Place them as they grow: Hold a large flower stem (wired and taped) at the base with thumb and forefinger, and slowly revolve it, watching the flower head until you see the most graceful position, then place it in the bouquet at this angle. Let some flowers look up (to the sky), some look to the right, some to the left and some cascade directly out in front close to the rim, but slightly off-center. Now your flowers will show sides as well as faces and will appear fresh and natural.

The importance of leaves: Leaves make the arrangement natural appearing and, by contrast, make the flowers more colorful and graceful. Use several types of leaves if possible. Notice the variety of foliage used in the color photographs. The addition of leaves can't be over-estimated in dried bouquets any more than in fresh ones. Fresh flowers, of course, already have leaves as part of the stem, so the addition of leaves in dried bouquets becomes even more important.

Use odd numbers: Your most dominant, or largest flowers, should vary in size and, if possible, be uneven in number. Use in groups of 3, 5, 7, etc.

Concealing the mechanics: the mechanics will be concealed with the layer of German statice on the Oasis. If the container is crystal, you will find it necessary to place a bowl insert or liner (anchoring it with clay) in which Oasis has been glued, so the crystal is clear and sparkling. See the large Pink Arrangement in Glass Vase, p. 96. Before the flowers are added, green filler material such as goldenrod and mahonia leaves, etc. are placed both to establish height, width and line and to form a background for the wired flower stems. When the arrangement is completed, place it in front of you and turn it slowly from all angles to see that your mechanics are concealed. If a wire sticks out at some point, you may be able to bend it back in or it may be easier to snip it off and tuck a leaf or piece of statice over it. A few leaves around the edge or a cluster of green goldenrod may add the finishing touch.

The light and airy look: A beautiful mass bouquet includes variations of flower sizes, flower forms and the illusion of freshness. Briefly:

Flower height: No two flowers should be placed at exactly the same height.

Flower size: Flowers should graduate in size from smallest flowers and buds at highest points to the largest and more fully open flowers near center, close to rim.

Flower forms: Flowers should alternate using some round, densely petaled flowers such as roses, carnations, marigolds, zinnias, etc. with some open-petaled flowers like tulips, lilies, daisies, etc. As contrast, use spike forms such as delphinium, larkspur, or blue salvia and foliage such as mahonia, artemesia, goldenrod and fern tips, etc.

GUIDE LINES FOR BEGINNERS

"Guide Lines" are little sketches showing the basic line to use. Most beginners will benefit greatly if they select one of these guidelines, sketch it on paper, and then plan what flower and leaf materials to use for the lines or spike forms, the round and focal point flowers, and the extra greenery to be used for filler material.

The symmetrical triangle is one where the main line is centered and identical lines radiate from the sides quite evenly. The arrangement may be one-sided or in-the-round. See Small Round Centerpiece, p. 50; Colonial Eagle Bowl, p. 72, Dolphin Candlesticks, p. 107.

The asymmetrical triangle is one where the center line is curved but tip end is centered and the radiating lines on each side are **not** identical. This guide line is used more frequently for one sided arrangements. See: The Modern Branch and Peony, p. 102; Gift From Your Garden, p. 104; Blue Delft Jar, p. 84.

The high triangle is high and delicate at the top and can be either narrow or wide at the base. It can be symmetrical or asymmetrical and is used for both one-sided and in-the-round arrangements. See: Antique Glass Vase, p. 96; Peonies and Pussywillows, p. 114.

The oval is one of radiating lines both above the rim of the container and below it, though the lower lines are shorter. It is frequently used to create a feeling of movement and motion. It is not easy to find dried materials to do this, since they are usually too stiff. Dried pussywillows, for instance, can be bent before drying and would be a good oval line choice, as would eucalyptus stems, basil herb stems, etc.

The fan is a series of arranged lines frequently used in one-sided 18th century arrangements such as those for the Delft Bricks, p. 88, and the Five Finger Posey Holder, p. 92. Slender, delicate leaves used to delineate the graduated lines are excellent and give a light, airy appearance.

The diamond, used for centerpieces, is a series of 3 triangles. Looking down, 2 triangles are fused together at the widest ends and a third-dimensional triangle is centered, standing on it's point. Following these lines, a centerpiece is simple to put together. See Pastel Low Centerpiece, p. 51; Centerpiece of Yellows, p. 58; and Centerpiece With Plate, p. 64.

Spiraling and zigzagging are terms frequently used in my instructions and can be easily visualized in these diagrams. The in-the-round bouquet is usually made in spirals, while a one-sided bouquet uses the zigzag or off-center placement.

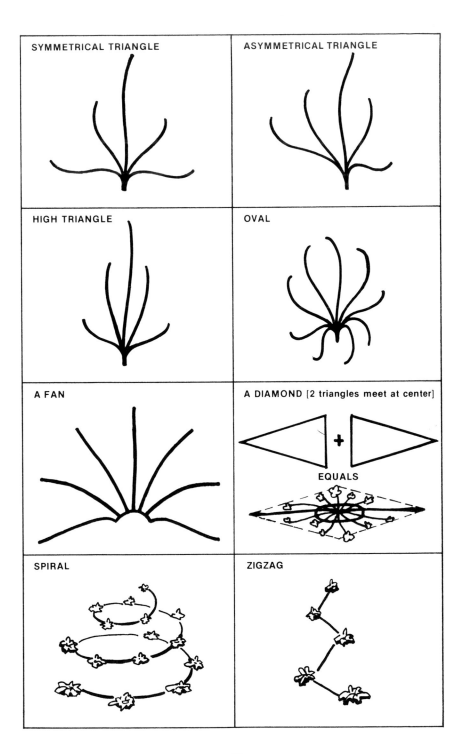

SYMMETRICAL TRIANGLE

ASYMMETRICAL TRIANGLE

HIGH TRIANGLE

OVAL

A FAN

A DIAMOND [2 triangles meet at center]

EQUALS

SPIRAL

ZIGZAG

Selecting
the right container

Every flower arranger should collect a selection of fine flower containers that enhance the rooms they will be used in. They can be antiques, good reproductions, or fine examples of country French, English or modern. They may be wood, pewter, silver, brass, glass, china, porcelain or pottery, but they should harmonize and compliment the room furnishings and should be partially exposed in the finished bouquet.

It amazes me at times when I find a beautiful bouquet made in a container that is in conflict with the room colors, the flowers, and is in just plain poor taste. You would not buy a Monet or an original Currier and Ives and then frame it in a dime store frame. The same is true of a lovely, decorative bouquet of flowers.

The type of container is determined by where it will be used. For a low centerpiece, you will need a selection of low, round or oval bowls. You'll need other types for one-sided mantel arrangements, hall tables and coffee tables. Begin to collect a container "wardrobe" that fits well in different rooms in your home. There is no doubt that a container with good line and proportion, plain in design and of good color, will make a finished bouquet lovelier.

Crystal or glass containers are excellent, too, but must be handled so the crystal is not shadowed by the Oasis and mechanics used in the arrangement. This can be accomplished by using a pewter candle collar (see p. 35) fastened in the vase with white clay or by using a pewter colored bowl liner set in the bowl so the mechanics will not be much in evidence. Vases with very small openings may have a plastic top from a spray can fastened in the top with clay or tape, and the arrangement is made entirely in this, leaving the crystal sparkling. A small custard cup can be fitted into the top of a glass container to support the mechanics, arranging leaves and filler material to disguise it. The photograph shows some good examples of different types of containers.

Top Row: Reproduction "Eagle" Bowl, Tôle Compote, Delft Oval Dish, Revere-Type Compote.

4th Row: Silver Bowl, Alabaster Compote, Delft Boscobel Bowl, Dolphin Candlestick, Footed Compote.

3rd Row: Delft Vase, Candle Collar, Dishcross, Pottery Vase, Silver Monteith.

2nd Row: Yellow Oval Bowl, Delft Vase, Pewter Cup, Crystal Bowl.

Bottom Row: Porcelain Bisque, Wooden Footed Compote, Pewter Bi-Centennial Punch Bowl.

Collecting the needed supplies

It is extremely frustrating and time-consuming to be without the right "tools" for making dried bouquets, and the lack of one simple ingredient may cause a disaster. The right wire weight, the kind of glue needed to anchor Oasis firmly, and a good pair of shears and pliers are as necessary as the flowers. Here is a suggested list.

Floral Wire: Wire is sold by weight and number. The heaviest wire has lower numbers and lightest wire has higher numbers. Most arrangers need a half pound each of #18 (heavy), #20 (medium) and #22 (light). Corsage weight is #26 and is good for miniatures.

Long Nose Pliers: My single most important tool, 6" long, plastic handled to prevent slipping, with sharp wire-cutter so they can be used both to cut wire stems and place them in bouquets. Placing flower stems with pliers prevents a lot of breakage.

Clay ["Cling"]: A green or white plastic clay. Can be used rolled or stretched to thin strip, placed around needlepoint holder to secure it. Used to anchor 2 parts of container together. Numerous uses for Cling.

Bowl Inserts: Are required when using crystal bowls to hold Oasis and conceal mechanics and for large bowls to make it easier to keep arrangement within space limitations. Adapters include small custard cups, metal tops from aerosol cans and pewter candle collars.

Oasis: Dry, rectangular brick of green floral foam easily pierced with wire and filler material.

Oasis Glue: Brushed on Oasis or directly on container to anchor Oasis.

Davee Tape: Green or white adhesive-like tape to secure Oasis to container with thin band.

Needlepoint Holders: Secure in container with Cling; press Oasis on pins.

Shears: Should be sharp enough to cut both flowers and wire with slender point.

DuPont's Cement: Clear, quick-drying glue for refastening petals and reinforcing flowers.

Sobo Glue: To fasten petals, fabric, ribbon, invitation and flowers in wedding pictures.

Sand and Buckshot: Clean, dry sand and coarse shot are nice to weight containers to prevent tipping over.

Petalspray: Special spray for dried flowers, forms tough protective coating against moisture damage.

Petalast: For preserving and storing flowers and bouquets. Add to security boxes for "insurance"

Security Boxes: Store flowers upright in airtight plastic boxes with thin sheet styrofoam and ½ c. Petalast.

Floratape: ½" wide stemwrap stretchable treated paper tape to lengthen and create wire stems. Comes in olive, twig, white, brown, spring green.

The mechanics
of stemming,
glueing
and spraying
for lasting beauty

Florataping Made Easy, Step-by-Step

Glueing to Reinforce Petals

Spraying Flowers with Petalspray

Florataping made easy
Step-by-step

The one skill you must acquire to make good dried arrangements is that of placing stretchable floratape over flower stems and wires to make artificial stems. When your wire stems are taped with olive green floratape, they can be curved or bent so they appear to be real. Florataping is, at first, difficult and it will help to practice.

FLORATAPING SINGLE FLOWERS

Use olive green floratape for a natural stem.

Step 1
Hold rose in left hand with short wire (or natural stem) protruding from flower. Place a 6"–12" (or longer) #22 wire against first wire, overlapping the two.

Step 2
Now you are holding both flower and wire in left hand. With right hand, place cut edge of floratape over top of the two wires and under back. Firm tape by pinching with right thumbnail and forefinger, holding stem in right hand.

Step 3

Hold left 1st and 2nd fingers *horizontally* behind the two wires with thumb on top, tape stretched between them. The tape should be taut so it stretches as you go. Spin wire and tape clockwise with right thumb and forefinger. Left hand holds wire, stretches tape, moving down the stem to cover wire. A smooth stem results.

Step 4

When about half the wire is covered with tape, pull your right hand with wire away from your left hand, *tearing* the tape off. Give an extra spin to secure tape edge to wire for a smooth, tight hold. *Do not tape to end of wire;* tape only that part of wire that will show. (Untaped wire penetrates Oasis more easily).

FLORATAPING FLOWERS ON STEMS

Step 5

Where flower stems are hollow, you may insert a wire into stem. Larkspurs require # 22 wire, delphinium may require # 20 or # 18 depending on length and heaviness of stems.

Step 6

If you cannot insert wire into stems, hold extending wire against 1″ of stem in left hand. Place cut edge of floratape on top of the two with cut edge pointing to left and running under back. Now firm tape by pinching with right thumb and forefinger.

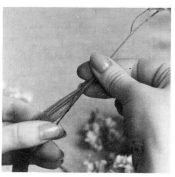

Step 7

Hold left 1st and 2nd fingers *horizontally* behind the two stems with thumb on top, tape stretched taut between them. Tape should be taut so it stretches as you go. With right thumb and forefinger, spin wire and tape clockwise, moving down as you cover wire. Tape only 1″–3″ of stem to hold wire securely.

Step 8

Pull right hand with wire away from left hand, tearing off tape; give torn edge an extra few spins to secure it to the wire. *Do not cut tape with scissor*—a tighter hold will result by tearing.

Lengthening Stems:

If a very long stem is needed for a big bouquet, tape stem to within 2" of end of wire; place piece of #18 wire against this and tape over the two, extending to needed length.

FLORATAPING LEAVES

Step 9

Rose Leaves: Floratape ½" tip end of 6" #22 wire to make a soft hold, then place dried leaflet against this. Floratape over the two; see steps 6–8. If leaf breaks, glue it in bouquet.

Step 10

Lily of Valley Leaves: Leaves are very brittle. Proceed as for rose leaves, placing taped tip of #22 wire 6" long on short natural stem end. Or glue leaves into bouquet.

Step 11

Peony Leaves: Preserve peony leaflets early in season. Insert #22 wire of desired length into stem end; see steps 5–8.

41

Step 12

Ferns: Shorten wild *yarrow fern* ends, then place #22 wire 6″ long against 1″ of spine. *Leatherleaf ferns:* cut leaflets from large stems, wire and tape each; follow steps 5–8.

Step 13

Mahonia: Leaves are glycerine-pre-served. Cut ends with 5, 7, 11 leaflet clusters. Wire and tape using steps 5–8 with 6″–12″ #18 or #20 wire. Fill in backs of one-sided bouquets with cut off ends. *Beech, forsythia, birch,* etc. may be used.

FLORATAPING FLOWER CLUSTERS

Step 14

Lily of Valley: Hold 3–5 stems of irregu-lar lengths, breaking stems at base even-ly. Hold cluster of stems at cut edge in left hand, place #22 wire 6″ long against ½″ of stem end; follow steps 6–8.

Step 15

Blue or White Salvia: Hold 2, 3 or 5 stems of irregular length totaling 5″ long with stem ends broken off evenly. Hold cluster in left hand, follow steps 6–8 using #22 wire 6″–12″ long. If bouquet is high, stems can be longer.

Step 16
Globe Amaranths: Stems are usually 5″ long. Cluster 3–5 stems, leaving them as long as possible, in irregular lengths, with stem ends even. Use #22 wire 6″–12″ long; follow steps 6–8.

Step 17
Immortelles: Break off woody gray stems 3″–5″ long; discard. Tape each stem cluster to #20 wire 6″–12″ long (or longer); see steps 6–8. Wiring stems permits easier placement in bouquets.

Step 18
Starflowers and Floral Butts: Pull them out by heads from bunch. Use 5–15 starflowers or 3–5 butts in clusters. Pull flowers to different lengths totaling 3″–5″; break off stem ends even. Follow steps 6–8.

Step 19
Green Goldenrod and Acacia: Break off 3 or more small sprays of goldenrod or short lateral stems or tip end of *Acacia* to 4″–6″ in length. (Longer if needed.) Clusters can be backed with tip of *leather-leaf fern* (glycerined). Use #20 wire, using desired length following steps 6–8. Tape thick clusters twice.

Step 20
Acroclinium: Hold 2–3 everlastings of different sizes and stem lengths totaling about 5″ long to make clusters. Break stem ends even. Follow steps 6–8, using # 22 wire 6″–12″ (or longer).

Step 21
Anemones: Stems with flower, buds and leaves can be preserved and extended by wire insertion; see steps 5–8. *Or* cut off stems to make shorter clusters of flowers and buds. Use # 22 wire 6″ long or longer.

FLORATAPING TO EXTEND STEMS
Step 22
Delphinium: Stems are hollow and quite straight. Cut stem as short as possible, insert # 18 wire, first taping tip of wire so it will not break through stem. Insert wire as far into stem as possible. Floratape where wire extends from stem, steps 5–8.

Step 23
Plume or Crested Celosia: Break celosia stems to 3″–5″ long. Force # 20 wire into woody stem end, about 1″ or more. If it will not penetrate, tape following steps 6–8, taping over stems a second time to insure tight hold.

GLUEING TO REINFORCE PETALS

Roses and Zinnias: Hold flowers upside down, run a thin "ribbon" of Dupont's cement around petals where attached to stems. Spread glue out on backs of petals with toothpick. Let flowers dry face down; turn face up. Glueing reinforces petals so they stay in place longer and withstand damage.

Lilies: Lilies are **extremely delicate** to handle. Hold flower in left hand, run Dupont's cement around back, spreading it out evenly with fingertip or toothpick on back of petals to 1½". This gives added strength to petals. If a petal breaks off, re-glue it back in place.

Bachelor Buttons, Marigolds, Carnations: Many-petaled flowers shrink in the calyx or "cup" which holds them, and after drying they are loose. Squirt a small amount of glue into this cup, turning the flower clockwise as you do so until it is filled with glue. When dried, glue will hold petals firmly in place and avoid shattering.

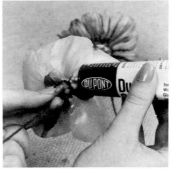

Peonies: Especially Single and Japanese peonies may collapse after being in a bouquet for some time. To avoid this, squirt a little glue near base on large overlapping petals about 1" from stem end, glueing two or three petals together. Do not use glue where it will show. Turn flower face down until dry; then face up.

SPRAYING FLOWERS WITH PETALSPRAY

Petalspray forms a tough, protective coating reinforcing flower petals, leaves and stems and inhibiting re-absorption of moisture from damp, humid conditions. Humidity, dust and human petal-pinchers are problem areas for all dried flowers, so it is wise to take precautions in the form of glueing and spraying.

On one of my spring lecture series, ten bouquets traveled over 4,000 miles. They were in and out of the car and auditoriums in windy, wet weather and were exposed to overnight damp conditions en route. The only reason they still looked so good at the end of almost three months was due to glueing and *Petalspray.*

Spraying flowers to use in bouquets
Shake flowers gently to remove all Petalast crystals. Flowers should be completely dry with no moisture remaining in the calyx. Wire, tape and glue flowers, placing them upright on sheet of styrofoam. Shake Petalspray well, then hold can 8"–10" from flowers and spray lightly and evenly on bottom, sides and tops. Use 2 coats, letting each dry thoroughly. Cover nose and mouth with handkerchief to avoid inhaling vapor.

Spraying flowers before storing
Place flowers on 1" wire stems on styrofoam. Spray as above. Do not store until completely dry. Add ½ cup Petalast to each storage box before sealing.

Spraying completed bouquets
All bouquets should receive a light spraying when completed and prior to storing. Cover flower container with plastic wrap, then spray as for "Flowers To Use In Bouquets" above. Follow directions on Petalspray can.

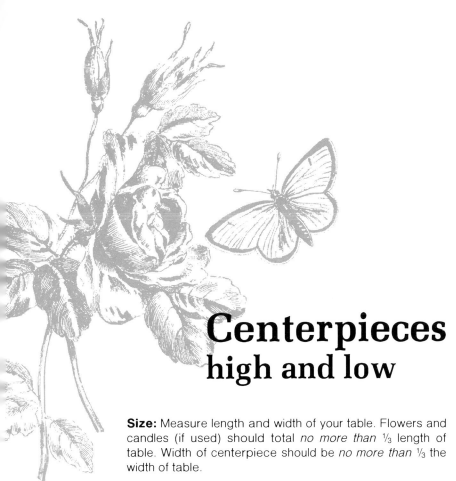

Centerpieces
high and low

Size: Measure length and width of your table. Flowers and candles (if used) should total *no more than* ⅓ length of table. Width of centerpiece should be *no more than* ⅓ the width of table.

Round or Oval: Table centerpieces need not be *oval* even though table is rectangular. With small table, using flowers and candles, it's preferable to use a round centerpiece to stay within space limitations.

Using Bowl Liners: Use with silver bowls needing polishing; with a very large bowl, smaller liner makes it easier to make a light, airy bouquet; use with glass containers to disguise mechanics.

The Low Centerpiece

Small Round Centerpiece
A Pastel Centerpiece
A Spring Basket of Flowers
A Fall Basket of Everlastings
A Centerpiece of Yellows
A Night In Vienna—Williamsburg Plate
Centerpiece With Matching Plate
A Pair of Bells or Baskets
Small Delft Arrangement

The High Decorative Centerpiece

Colonial Eagle Centerpiece
Redware Pot of Everlastings
The Decorative Large Bouquet
Country French Flowers

Small round centerpiece

See Color Photograph p. 15

This rose and blue arrangement can be made in an antiqued tin, china or Revere-type bowl about 4½"–5" in diameter. Both bowls shown are 4½" wide and 2½" high. The finished arrangement will measure: 2½-3 × 4½" = 11"–13" high and in-the-round.

You will need:
Oasis and glue
½ bch. German statice
Bunch green goldenrod
1 lg. leatherleaf fern cut into tips
1 small bch. blue and white annual statice
7 short stems pink, plume celosia
1 doz. short white larkspur stems
7 small-medium roses
2 doz. white acroclinium (daisy everlastings)
40 5" blue salvia stems
Large cluster pink pepperberries, cut up

Preparing the flowers:
Make 18 clusters goldenrod-fern tips; see Step 19, p. 43.
Make 9 clusters annual statice on 3" wire stems; follow Step 19, p. 43.
Stem celosia, Step 23, p. 44.
Extend larkspur to 11", Steps 5–8, p. 40.
Wire and tape roses, Steps 1–4, p. 39.
Glue and spray, p. 45–46.
Make 11 acroclinium clusters 9" long, Step 20, p. 44.
Make 13 7" long clusters salvia, Step 15, p. 42.
Make 9 small pepperberry clusters; follow Step 17, p. 43.

Alternate color selections, see p. 50

Putting it all together:

1. Cut 3″ square of Oasis, round top, sides and bottom to fit bowl; should be 1″ higher than rim. Brush bottom of Oasis generously with Oasis glue; press into bowl and weight until dry. Cut pile of 1½″ pieces German statice. Beginning around inside of bowl, insert statice as close to bottom as possible. Place pieces at top center; continue until Oasis is covered.

2. Place 3 goldenrod-fern clusters at top center to form triangle at heights of 9″, 10″, 11″. Add shorter clusters around center and all sides extending out about 3″–4″ to give background. Add blue and white statice deep in bouquet between goldenrod clusters for depth and contrast.

3. Place few plumey celosia tips deep at center, others gracefully at sides. (Plumes can be cut into pieces if too large.) Add larkspur, inserting stems to extend out 2″ beyond other flowers. Insert 3 near top in open triangle at 11″–13″, spiral others to lower sides, see Main Axis p. 30.

4. Place small rosebud at top center at 11". Spiral remaining roses with largest ones near rim of bowl. Place these with pliers; do not bury them too deeply. Add white acroclinium and blue salvia clusters, spiraled in bouquet.

5. Add pepperberries last (they are so delicate). Overlap statice and goldenrod where possible to keep berries farthest out. You can dip clusters in glue and glue in if you wish. When completed, cover bowl with plastic wrap, spray bouquet lightly, see Spraying p. 46.

Alternate Color-Flower Combinations: You may omit some and add others

Yellow/Blue/Apricot	Green/White/Blue	Pink/Red/White
First 3 ingredients plus:	First 3 ingredients plus:	First 3 ingredients plus:
Leatherleaf ferntips	Mahonia leaf tips	Mahonia leaf tips
Yellow annual statice	White annual statice	White annual statice
White larkspur or blue delphinium (Conn. Yankees)	Blue delphinium (Conn. Yankees) or white larkspur	Short pink astible or plume celosia
Orange plume celosia	Small green zinnias or marguerites or carnations	Pink or white larkspur
Yellow or apricot-nectar roses or zinnias	Blue salvia clusters	Small pink zinnias or red tulips or carnations
Yellow acroclinium or immortelles or mini-daffodils	Baby's breath clusters	"Gypsy" rosebuds or small "Tropicana" buds
Orange globe amaranth		White acroclinium or anemones

A pastel centerpiece

See Color Photograph p. 17

This pastel centerpiece is made in a Williamsburg Delft oval bowl on a pewter dishcross. Bowl is 7″ long, 4″ wide, 3″ high plus 2″ for dishcross. Using largest dimension figure: 2½–3 x 7″ = 18″–21″ long; 13″ wide at center; 13″–15″ in height.

You will need

Oasis
Bunch German statice
9 mahonia leaves
15 goldenrod stems
Leatherleaf fern tips
15 pieces acacia
18 blue delphinium, Conn. Yankees
9 pink and apricot roses
10 yellow and apricot tulips
36 blue salvia stems
36 lily of valley stems
5–6 lily of valley leaves

Preparing the flowers

Tape mahonia leaves, Step 13, p. 42
Prepare goldenrod-fern and acacia, Step 19 p, p. 43; blue salvia and lily of valley, Steps 14 & 15, p. 42
Extend short delphinium stems to 6″–12″, see Steps 5–8, p. 40–41
Glue tulips and roses, see Glueing p. 45. Wire & tape, Steps 1–4, p. 39–40. Place upright on styrofoam.
Spray all flowers lightly 2 coats, see Spraying p. 46.

Alternate Flower-Color Combinations p. 54.

Putting it all together:

1. Invert bowl on Oasis to mark impression; cut to fit. Place an additional ½" thick piece Oasis or ½" clean sand in bottom of bowl for extra height, then press Oasis into bowl extending over rim about 1". Round off top and sides. Place small piece Cling on center of dishcross to anchor bowl.

2. With shears, snip off generous pile 1½"–3" pieces German statice. Beginning at rim, insert statice all around edge. Place several pieces on top center of Oasis, then overlap statice down to first row. Repeat until Oasis is covered.

3. Place 3 mahonia leaves in center open triangle at 10" height. Add one leaf little lower to left of center and second leaf right of center. Reverse bowl and repeat on opposite side, making leaves go left, then right, zigzagging across center. Place 2 longer leaves extending outward about 7", one on each side.

4. Place 3 goldenrod-fern clusters at top center inside leaf triangle. Add several clusters at each end, extending over each mahonia leaf. Add remaining clusters here and there as shown to give depth and background.

5. Add two or three sprays acacia at top center to 13″ high. Add some to right and left and two sprays extending out at each end over mahonia leaves. Hold unused sprays; use to fill in any spaces when bouquet is completed.

6. Place blue delphinium stems, the first three most delicate ones in a top center triangle about 13″ high. Then, one each larger flowered, longer stemmed sprays at the ends, extending over mahonia and acacia. Place three more closer to center at each end. Add several at sides near center, extending these outward at rim.

7. Place rosebud near top center, then another near top, off-center. Add rose at farthest ends inside delphinium tips; add tulip at opposite end. Alternate roses and tulips, placing largest flowers near center rim on each side. Work from side to side; avoid exact duplication.

8. Add lily of valley and salvia clusters, some at top center at 14" high, and some near rim at sides, a few near ends. These spike forms add color and interest. Tuck in few lily of valley leaves wherever possible, extended out for textural contrast. When bouquet is complete, spray lightly, see Spraying p. 46.

Alternate Color-Flower Combinations: You may omit some and add others.

Pink and Blue

First 5 ingredients plus:

Baby's breath

Blue delphinium-Conn. Yankees, short stems

Pink and rose roses

Pink and rose carnations (small) or green zinnias

Blue salvia

Red, White and Blue

First 5 ingredients plus:

White annual statice

White larkspur

Blue delphinium-Conn. Yankees, short stems

"Tropicana" or "Gypsy" rosebuds, dyed red immortelles or celosia

Daisies or white zinnias or white straw-flowers or large blue cornflowers

Yellow, White, Apricot

First 5 ingredients plus:

Yellow annual statice

White Conn. Yankee delphinium or white larkspur (short stems)

Yellow and apricot roses

Yellow carnations or marigolds or green zinnias

Anemones, or yellow acroclinium or daisies

A spring basket
See Color Photograph p. 15.

A fall basket of everlastings
See Color Photograph p. 2.

This spring-like dried arrangement is a small centerpiece which could be used on a coffee or end table. Make several for party centerpieces. Basket is 9" wide 9" to handle top, 9" across. Arrangement should show some of basket, so figure: 2 x 9" = 18" in length, 9" at high point, and 9" across. Fall Basket, see alternate p. 57.

You will need

Oasis and glue

German statice

Green goldenrod

1–2 leatherleaf fern cut in tips

7 small poppy pods with stems

5 yellow immortelle clusters

24 orange globe amaranth

36 yellow acroclinium

3 small-med. yellow tulips

3 miniature daffodils

Preparing the flowers

Make 13 clusters goldenrod-fern tips, Step 19, p. 43

Insert wire into 5" poppy stems; extend to 12".

Stem immortelles, Step 17, p. 43

Cluster acroclinium 9" long, Step 20, p. 44

Make 13 clusters amaranths 2–3 per stem to 8" long, Step 16, p. 43

Wire-tape tulips and daffodils 6"–8" long, Steps 1–4, p. 39–40.

Stand upright on styrofoam; spray all flowers, see Spraying, p. 46.

Fall Basket-see Alternate p. 57.

Putting it all together:

1. Cut oval piece of Oasis 3" x 2" x 1¼"; taper top and sides. (For larger basket, increase or double size). Brush bottom generously with Oasis glue, place in basket, weight until dry. OR, place floral clay on bottom of oval needlepoint holder, place in basket, top with Oasis.

2. Cut pile of German satice 1½"–3" long. Cover Oasis at bottom and sides first, then work from top down until Oasis is covered.

3. Place 3 goldenrod-fern clusters in a triangle in center to height of 9", placing each piece slightly shorter than preceding one. Add more shorter clusters in center of basket, some near handles and some extending out beyond basket at each end to total length of 18". If needed, insert more unwired green goldenrod.

4. Place poppy pods at top center in wide-open triangle extending outward. Stems are interesting and should extend beyond basket. Place pod at each end with a couple on each side. Place immortelles deep in arrangement with several near center and one each near far ends.

5. Place several clusters of globe amaranths and acroclinium, first at top center extending slightly above handle, with other clusters extending out over fern at far ends and a few at sides.

6. Place the three tulips in an open triangle, one tulip about 7" in height near center, others low at each end. Place daffodils between tulips. Finish placing all amaranths and acroclinium. Spray bouquet, see Spraying, p. 46.

A FALL BASKET OF EVERLASTINGS (p.2). Follow above directions using larger basket: make twice as long as basket & slightly higher than handle. Fill with: lotus pods, dried grasses, Mahonia, fern, orange globe amaranths, acroclinium, statice & "mushroom" pods.

A centerpiece of yellows

See Color Photograph p. 17.

This low, oval yellow bowl is 10" long, 5½" wide and 3½" high. Using largest dimension of 10", it would measure: 2½–3 x 10" = 25"–30" long, 15" across at center, 13"–14" at highest point.

You will need

Block of Oasis
Bunch German statice
25 green goldenrod stems
3 lg. leatherleaf ferns
25 5"–7" pieces acacia
9 med. "Jan de Graff" yellow and orange lilies
9 med. yellow marigolds
36 orange globe amaranths
30 white Japanese anemones
5 anemone leaves, 3–4"
Butterfly, optional

Substitute flowers, see p. 60.

Preparing the flowers

Make goldenrod-fern tip clusters, Step 19, p. 43, and 25 acacia stems
Make 15 amaranth clusters, Step 16, p. 43.
Make 13 anemone clusters, Step 21, p. 44. Stem anemone leaves, see Rose leaves, Step 9, p. 41.
Glue marigolds and lilies, see Glueing p. 45. Wire and tape to 10" long, Steps 1–4, p. 39–40. Stand upright on styrofoam.
Spray all flowers 2 coats Petalspray; see Spraying p. 46.

Putting it all together:

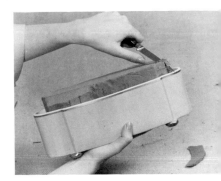

1. Fit block of Oasis into the bowl so it fits snugly. Shave edges to round top and sides. If Oasis is loose, glue, weight and dry. OR place thin strip Davee tape diagonally from one side to other, securing tape to edge of bowl. Oasis should extend 1″ above rim.

2. Snip large bunch German statice into 1½″–3″ pieces. Beginning at bowl rim, insert statice all around edge. Insert several pieces at top center, then overlap statice down to first row. Repeat until Oasis is covered.

3. Place 3 goldenrod-fern clusters in open triangle at center to height of 9″. Continue adding shorter clusters around these, placing several deep in center of triangle. Place some at the sides and extend some out 4″ at each end of bowl. Add acacia extending 6″ at each end and 12″ high at center top.

4. Add small lily at top center and on either end with one large lily extending out from edge of bowl front off-center on each side. Avoid making sides identical; use some lilies in approximately, but not exactly, identical positions.

5. Begin to add marigolds at each side near top center to 13" high; then zigzag marigolds at each side down to rim, spacing flowers 3" apart; last flower on each side should be a little below bowl rim. Add clusters of globe amaranths, keeping them in areas where no larger flowers have been placed and extending them out beyond other flowers in a 2 layer effect. Add 2 or 3 sprays near top center then add all remaining sprays.

6. Add anemone clusters, keeping them out and away from other flowers so they form an airy white halo. Place delicate spray with buds at top center, then cluster them here and there, but do not place too deeply. Add a few larger anemone leaves near rim for visual weight. Glue on butterfly. Wrap bowl in plastic wrap; spray bouquet lightly, see Spraying p. 46.

Flower Substitutions:

For Acacia: Substitute orange plume celosia.

For Marigolds: Yellow or apricot carnations or immortelle clusters.

For Anemones: Small green zinnias or white strawflowers or yellow acroclinium or yellow immortelles.

For Anemone leaves: Small peony leaflets or tip ends of mahonia leaves or glycerined leatherleaf fern tips.

A night in Vienna
With Williamsburg "Colonial Sprays" China
See Color photograph p. 3

A party for a music-minded group using a violin for the centerpiece container to carry out a waltz theme. The china is part of the theme—in this case the Colonial Williamsburg Wedgwood china called, "Colonial Sprays" decorated with bicolor tulips and rosebuds. These flowers are repeated in the violin spray arrangement with lovely light and deep blue delphinium.

The length and width of the flower spray can be as large or small as your table dictates. Allow enough space for candlesticks, too. The flowers should be about 6" high at the center and delphinium should extend out to the right side at top and to left side at bottom, as shown.

You will need
Violin; small piece Oasis
½ bch. white annual statice
#20 and #22 wire, floral tape
20 or more rose leaflets
5 stems light & dark blue single delphinium 8"–10" long
6 pink roses; 1 rose bud
3 large yellow tulips
2 small yellow tulips
DuPont Cement

Preparing your flowers:
Break off small florets of white statice from stems

Wire & tape half the rose leaves, see Step 9 p. 41 on #22 wire about 3"–8" long. Reserve others.

Wire & tape delphinium, see Step 22 p. 44, extending stems to 12" long on #20 wire.

Wire & tape roses, see Steps 1–4, p. 39–40 using #20 wire 6" long; tape bud 10" long.

Wire & tape tulips using #20 wire as for roses, taping largest 3" long; 2 small ones 6" long.

Putting it all together:

1. Cut Oasis 1″ thick, 2″ wide, 4″ long; cut in half crosswise and slide each piece under strings on each side of the "bridge". Place 1″ thick, rounded topped piece Oasis over first pieces; anchor with short, bent piece of wire.

2. Cover Oasis completely with statice florets, inserting them into Oasis. Insert rose leaves 5″ long at right top and 6″ long at bottom left. Add shorter leaves at center to form lazy S line. Reserve others.

3. Place 2 stems delphinium at top right side in delicate curve. Place 3 stems extended from Oasis to left side at bottom of violin.

4. Place rosebud 5″ shorter than the delphinium stem at top right. Add rose leaves near bud stem; glue leaflets to the stem itself. Add another rose near base of violin off-center; glue leaves to stem. Add rose on left side just above center.

5. Place small tulips, one at top right and one at bottom left sides as shown. Place 3 large tulips in center cluster: one faces left, one faces right, one looks up. Glue in more rose leaves around them.

6. Place roses near tulips to left or right; tulips should be higher than roses. Avoid a flat, all one level appearance. Glue in delphinium florets where space permits.

Alternate Color & Flower Combination:

In place of delphinium, substitute white, pink or blue larkspur or plume celosias, or delicate sprays of green leaves or silver artemesia. Use medium sized peach or pink zinnias, large roses, carnations, or pale crested celosia in place of tulips. Pink miniature strawflowers may be used in place of roses.

Centerpiece with matching plate

See Color Photograph p. 6

This lovely centerpiece of pink, whites and blue flowers was chosen to compliment the blue-bordered plate with flower center. Deep rose candles bring out the rosey color in peonies. The bowl is an oval white unglazed porcelain, 4" high and 10" long. Using the largest dimension of 10" (length) x 2½–3 = 25"–30" finished length from leaf tips on each side, and 15" across at the center, and about 13" high at highest point, measured from table top. Read "The Diamond" in GUIDELINES p. 32 and 33.

You will need

Oasis block and oasis glue

1 bch. German statice

1–2 bch. green goldenrod in 24 clusters

12 short stems glycerined green Mahonia leaves

15 short stems delphinium, 6"–8" long, light & dark blue

10 pink to rose single Japanese peonies 3"–5" in size; include 1 bud

40 stems white anemone Japonica with leaves & buds in 15 clusters

12 clusters Baby's breath

Butterfly

Preparing the flowers:

Cut German Statice 1½"–3" long.

Make goldenrod clusters, Step 19 p. 43.

Wire & tape mahonia leaf ends, Step 13, p. 42 using # 18 wire cut 6" long. Stems should be 11" to 13".

Extend delphinium stems as Step 22, p. 44 to total lengths of 10"–12".

Wire & tape peonies to # 18 wire, 10"–12" long. Glue, p. 45; spray, p. 46.

Cluster anemone flowers on 5" stems, with leaves, buds: see Step 21, p. 44 using # 20 wire. Make them 10"–12" long.

Wire & tape Babys breath clusters on # 20 wire, making them 8"–10".

Putting it all together:

1. Using paring knife, make Oasis into oval shape, rounding top and sides to fill about ⅔ of bowl. There will be space all around Oasis, see picture. Spread tbsp. Oasis glue in bottom of bowl; press oasis firmly on it; dry. (Or use needlepoint holder).

2. Cover sides first, then Oasis top with small statice pieces. Add 3 clusters goldenrod at top center forming open triangle 10″ in ht. Place 3 clusters at each end of bowl extending out 3″–5″. Fill in center & sides with shorter clusters.

3. Add 3 mahonia leaves, repeating center triangle and placing leaves deeper in bouquet and shorter than goldenrod. Place 2 longer stems, one at each side extended out 6″ from bowl. Place short leaflet at front center near rim; repeat on reverse side. Use remaining leaves deep in bouquet.

4. Place 3 delphinium stems at top center to ht. of 11"–13" to form an irregular triangle extending out higher than goldenrod. Add 1 stem at each end extended out above mahonia leaves. Place short deep blue stem off-center near bowl rim in front; repeat on other side. Reserve some delphinium.

5. Place peony bud at top center in delphinium triangle, about 13" high. Add 3 more medium peonies 3"–5" lower in triangle shape. Place peony at each end about 3" out from bowl edge, then 2 largest, deeply colored peonies at side centers close to or overhanging bowl rim. Use others where space permits.

6. Place Anemone clusters here and there extending 2"–5" out from other flowers for light, airy effect. Add Baby's breath with remaining delphinium wherever needed.

Butterfly: Cut butterfly lengthwise through paper body; hold together, place small amount glue on cut edges and place on flower in lighting position.

A pair of bells or baskets

See Color Photograph p. 16

The old milk glass bells were originally used over gaslights to protect the ceiling and may be found in antique shops. You may also use the covers from small bowls, glass or ceramic dishes, resting them sideways on knobs for balance. *For baskets,* use small ones placed sideways back to back with the handles extended out at each side and flowers placed under and over them. The double arrangement may be centered on a mantel or used as a table centerpiece, or one used on each of a matching pair of tables. The bells are 5″ wide. Figure 5″ x 2½ = 12½″ from bell to farthest end (or less). When bells are placed back-to-back, flowers extend 25″ from tip to tip and 8″–10″ at highest point. (See sketch).

You will need:

Oasis, Oasis glue & DuPont Cement, wire & tape

½ bch. German statice

1 bch. green goldenrod

1 glycerined leatherleaf fern

14 short 5″–7″ stems light and dark blue delphihium, "Conn. Yankees"

18 med. peach roses ("Apricot Nectar")

14 Anemone Japonica stems 5″ long, with buds, leaves

24 rose leaflets

Preparing the flowers:

Wire & tape goldenrod, Step 19 p. 43, on # 20 wire cut 3″–6″ long.

Cut 7–8 side fronds from fern; tape each to 3″ long wire, see Step 12, p. 42.

Extend delphinium 5″–7″ longer, see Step 22, p. 44 taping on # 20 wire.

Tape 5″–11″ stems to roses, see Steps 1–4 p. 39–40 on # 20 wire. Glue, p. 45 and spray lightly, p. 46.

Wire & tape Anemone clusters (flowers, buds & leaves) on # 22 wire cut 5″–7″ in length. Step 21, p. 44.

Wire & tape ½ rose leaves, see Step 9, p. 41 on 2″ stems. Glue in all others.

Putting it all together:

1. Cut 2 round Oasis balls 2″ wide. Use Oasis glue generously in bottom of bell or basket, press Oasis ball into it firmly; dry. Repeat with other bell. Cover Oasis lightly with short pieces German statice.

2. Add green goldenrod starting at center with 3″ long stems, continue extending out at sides to about 9″ at longest points. Add fern tips around sides of bells. Add wired rose leaves.

3. *For each bell,* place longest delphinium stems extended 12″ out from center to side, follow with 2 shorter stems in each. Add 4 short stems at center of each. Flowers should reach out to *left* side on one bell, *right* side of other bell.

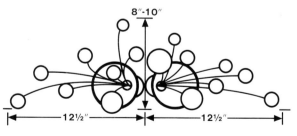

4. Place first rose at center of bell to ht. of 5″. Add 4 more roses in irregular row from center to farthest side. Place 2 larger roses in front and rear center. Place clusters of Anemones here and there. Glue in rose leaves. *Repeat with 2nd bell.* Place bells together; adjust where needed.

Small Delft arrangement

See Color Photograph p. 15.

The Blue Delft pot is 4″ high and the yellow, blue and white arrangement is made in-the-round. Figure height: 2½–3 x 4″ = 10″–12″ and 12″ at widest point.

You will need

Sand and Oasis

German statice

5 slender mahonia leaves

1 bch. green goldenrod

10 sprays white larkspur

36 stems blue saliva

3 miniature white carnations and buds

7 yellow immortelle clusters

6 small-med. yellow tulips

7 yellow or white daisies (marguerites)

20 5″ stems bachelor buttons

Preparing the flowers

Wire and tape short mahonia leaflets to 8″; see Step 13, p. 42.

Wire and tape 3 goldenrod clusters 9″ long and 10 clusters 6″ long, Step 19, p. 43.

Extend short stemmed larkspur tips to 12″, Steps 5–8, p. 40–41.

Make 12–15 salvia clusters 10″ long, Step 15, p. 42; and 7 immortelle clusters 7″ long; see Step 17, p. 43

Wire and tape carnations, tulips, daisies to 10″ long. Steps 1–4, p. 39–40. Place upright on styroform. Glue, p. 45, spray, p. 46.

Glue bachelor buttons p. 45. Wire and tape 8 clusters of 2 or 3 4″ stems extended to 8″, Step 16, p. 43. Spray, p. 46.

Alternate color selections p. 71

Putting it all together:

1. Fill bottom of pot with 1½" dry clean sand for weight. If omitted, container will be top-heavy. Cut piece of Oasis 5" x 3" x 3" and press on pot to mark opening; shave sides to fit snugly down to sand. Round off top at edge of pot on sides and about 1" above rim. Cut pile of 1½" pieces German statice, cover rim edge with statice, then cover from top down.

2. Place 3 mahonia leaf tips at center, extended out to form open-triangle about 8" high. Add 2 more leaflets lower down near base extending out gracefully. Add long clusters goldenrod at top center within leaf triangle at 12". Spiral shorter ones down and 4–5" out at sides. Place other short stems in center to fill space and cover mechanics.

3. Add larkspur; place longest stem in center near top at 12", then spiral down, *working in the round,* with 3–4 stems near base to form widest points of bouquet. Should keep it 12" round. Place salvia cluster near top, spiraling others. Keep stems long enough for flowers to extend out from bouquet.

4. Add carnation buds close to top, then place 3 8" stems deep in bouquet in widely spaced triangle. Whiteness will make other flowers more colorful. Some will overlap for dimension. Repeat using immortelles.

5. Place 6 tulips in zigzag starting from the top with smallest 13" high; add two more, one to left of center and one to right, close to rim. Reverse bowl; repeat on other side. Reach in with pliers to bend stems, making flowers look right or left, etc.

6. Place daisies with smallest near top below first tulip; spiral the remainder. Don't bury them—leave stems long enough so flowers will stand out in bouquet, few will hang over rim.

7. Place bachelor button clusters; start with 13" stem top center, then spiral down keeping intense blue color in a running line from top to rim. Fill in holes with salvia, remaining pieces goldenrod or leaves. Cover pot with plastic wrap, spray bouquet lightly; see Spraying p. 46.

Alternate Color-Flower Combinations

Pink and Blue

First 4 ingredients plus:

Blue Conn. Yankee delphinium

Pink strawflowers

White and pink roses

Baby's breath

Pink globe amaranths

Red/Gold/Blue

First 4 ingredients plus:

Blue Conn. Yankee delphinium or large florets

Blue annual statice

Gold marigolds or yarrow or red crested celosia

Tansy

Red roses

Yellow acroclinium

Yellow/Blue/Green

First 4 ingredients plus:

Conn. Yankee delphinium or large florets

Squirrel-tail grass

Yellow marigolds

Green zinnias

Yellow everlasting acroclinium or strawflowers

Green hill flowers, parsley, herbs

Colonial eagle centerpiece
See Color Photograph p. 5

This apricot, green and white decorative high centerpiece is made in-the-round in bowl measuring 8″ in diameter, 3″ high plus dishcross (5″ total). Using the largest dimension, arrangement will measure: 2½–3 x 8″ = 20″–24″ at highest point, 20″ in-the-round.

You will need
Oasis and glue
Bunch German statice
2 bch. green goldenrod
7 stems orange plume celosia
9 stems Bells of Ireland
12 "Apricot Nectar" roses
7 green zinnias "Envy"
13 white Conn. Yankee delphinium or white larkspur
40 stems yellow acroclinium
35 stems orange globe amaranth
1 doz. lily of valley leaves
Baby's breath

Flower substitutions, p. 74.

Preparing the flowers
Prepare clusters:
25 or more goldenrod clusters, 5″–12″ long, Step 19, p. 43.
17 acroclinium (2–3 each), Step 20 p. 44.
15 amaranth (3 each), Step 16, p. 43.
12 baby's breath (follow goldenrod) Step 19, p. 43.
Wire and tape lily of valley leaves, Step 10, p. 41.
Cut Bells of Ireland to 8″; extend to 16″, Step 5. p. 40.
Cut delphinium to 7″ long; tape and extend to 15″ long, Steps 5–8, p. 40–41.
Roses and zinnias: Wire and tape to stems 8″–14″; see Steps 1–4, p. 39–40. Place upright on styrofoam then glue, p. 45, and spray, p. 46.
Extend celosia stems, Step 23, p. 44.

Putting it all together:

1. Cut square of Oasis 5″ wide; slice off points; taper to rounded ball as high as possible. Pour about 1 teasp. Oasis glue in bowl bottom; press ball on this; weight until dry. Fasten dishcross to bowl with Cling. Cut pile of statice 1½″–3″ long. Insert short pieces low on sides of Oasis; cover completely.

2. Place plumey green goldenrod at top center to form triangle at 3 points about 15″ in height. Add shorter stems deep in center and place others extended out gracefully over edges of bowl to 5″ beyond rim. Fill in center. Place 1–2 celosia stems deep in center, remaining stems in spiral.

3. Place 3 bells of Ireland stems near top about 13″–15″ in height in center triangle, letting them emerge from Main Axis with tips waving. Spiral additional stems to rim; let them extend out 6″–8″. Bells add illusion of movement.

4. Now place first smallest rose at top center about 17″ high. Spiral remaining roses from top to rim, working in the round, with largest roses low near rim. Rose stems should be long enough to allow for graceful curves and bending.

5. Add 2–3 smallest green zinnias near top rose about 3" lower. Spiral remaining zinnias, keeping flowers separate and of different lengths. Avoid having them all the same distance from center— place some deeper in bouquet, others farther out.

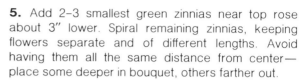

6. Place 3 delicate sprays delphinium at 19" or higher in center. Add cluster of acroclinium and 2 of amaranths and lily of valley leaf in the center, filling up center triangle. Place remaining delphinium, acroclinium, amaranth and valley leaves, keeping stems longer than roses and zinnias to extend out farther than larger flowers. This avoids "pincushion." Add baby's breath. Cover bowl with plastic wrap, spray p. 46

Flower Substitutions:

For Bells of Ireland: Light or deep blue delphinium, "Connecticut Yankee," curved pussywillows, dried basil stems, or young green curved stems wild dock or slender green cattail leaves.

For White Delphinium: White larkspur with green tips or pale blue delphinium or sprays of Bridlewreath shrub or White Deutzia shrub.

Green Zinnias: Green Lenten roses, yellow, white or apricot zinnias, clusters dried pachysandra.

"Apricot Nectar" Roses: Yellow or white roses or apricot African daisies (Gerbera type) or Coreopsis, Calendula, Tithonia.

Acroclinium: Yellow immortelle clusters or yellow mini strawflowers.

Baby's Breath: Green squirrel-tail grass or omit.

Redware pot of everlastings

See Color Photograph p. 18.

This arrangement is made in-the-round using an old redware pot—an excellent color with flowers. It is casual, light and airy and would be suitable for a family room or country kitchen table. The pot is 6″ high; height would be: $2\frac{1}{2}$–3 x 6″ = 15″–18″ and 18″ at widest point.

You will need

Oasis and sand

German statice

2 bch. green goldenrod

7 pheasant feathers

9 stems orange plume celosia

9 medium yarrow

7 stems blackbeard wheat

5 stems curly caustiz fern

3 doz. orange globe amaranth

6–7 sprays wild grape vine and 4–5 large grape leaves

Preparing the flowers

Cluster 25 stems goldenrod 5″–12″ long, Step 19, p. 43.

Tape pheasant feathers: 2 short curvy ones on #20 wire, extend to 12″ in length. Tape remaining feathers in circles, first cutting off quills; tape to 6″–8″ long. on #20 wire, see Steps 6–8, p. 40–41.

Pull tip of feather down, fasten with tape at quill end. See photo.

Fasten celosia to 10″–15″ #20 wire, Step 23, p. 44. Repeat above with yarrow and wheat. Cut caustiz in small sections; wire and tape each following Step 12, p. 42.

Make clusters of amaranths 8″–15″ long, Step 16, p. 43.

Tape stems of grape leaves with 8″ natural stems, extend to 14″–16″ on #20 wire. (Leaves are preserved in Petalast.) Wire and tape leaves to 5″, Step 9, p. 41.

Putting it all together:

1. Weight pot with 2" clean, dry sand. Press 4" x 4" x 6" piece of Oasis lengthwise on top to make impression, then cut to fit snugly down into sand, leaving top extended 1½" over rim. Round off edges. Cut pile German statice 1"–3" long; insert to cover edge of pot, then cover Oasis completely.

2. Place 3 longest goldenrod stems at center in triangle to height of 15"; spiral shorter goldenrod extending out 6" at sides, see Main Axis p. 30. Fill in center with goldenrod.

3. Place first straight feather near center at 17", second one extending from center to left forming two spikes. Place smallest circle-feather near top center at 16"; spiral remaining feathers extending out in *flat horizontal* circles near rim. Add orange celosia near top, zigzagging to rim, then reverse pot and repeat on other side.

4. Add yarrow, starting with small flower at top center at 18″ high; spiral others to rim. Add wheat, curly caustiz in same way, working in-the-round.

5. Add amaranth clusters; place first cluster high in center; concentrate remaining half of clusters in a loose line to rim, extending them out from other material. Place a cluster deep in bouquet, with another cluster almost on top of it, extended out. Reverse pot and repeat on other side.

6. Add grape stems last as they are easily damaged. Place with pliers, starting with delicate spray in center at 20″ in height. Place 3 more on sides in-the-round, extending far out from other materials. Place remaining ones near center of each side. Use grape leaves close to rim for visual weight. Spray bouquet, see Spraying p. 46

The decorative large bouquet

See Color Photograph p. 24

A high, decorative bouquet in red, white and blue requiring a large number of flowers. It could be scaled down to ⅔ the size using about half the number of flowers. The pewter compote is 5½" high and 8" wide. Take the larger measurement, figure: 2½–3 x 8" = 20"–24" high and 20"–24" in the round. This bouquet measures 25" high, 25" wide.

You will need:

One or more blocks Oasis
Liner bowl for compote or large needlepoint holder
Lg. bch. German statice
5 bch. green goldenrod
2 lg. bch. white statice
20 13" stems delphinium
9 4"–5" white Japanese peonies
15 med.-lg. red roses
3 doz. 10" long white larkspur stems
3 doz. bachelor buttons
13 blue echinops (thistle)
18 small-med. peony leaves
Large butterfly (optional)

Preparing the flowers:

Cluster goldenrod see Step 19, p. 43 use # 18 wire cut 8"–12" long.

Repeat above, use all white statice.

Extend delphinium stems Steps 5–8 p. 40–41 on # 18 wire, 3 stems 24" long, 9 stems 20", 8 stems 13".

Extend larkspur to 25" long, as above.

Wire & tape Peonies on # 18 wire 15"–19" long, Steps 1–4 p. 39–40 glue & spray p. 45 & p. 46.

Extend peony leaves to 15" see Step 11 p. 41.

Glue bachelor buttons p. 45; tape clusters of 3 5" long stems on # 20 wire, see Step 16 p. 43, 12"–20" long.

Extend 7" Echinops stems inserting # 18 wire to 15"–20" Step 23 p. 44.

Roses: Wire & tape on # 18 wire to 12"–20" long, see Steps 1–4 p. 39–40. Glue & spray p. 45 & 46.

Putting it all together:

1. Use liner-bowl as in "Country French Flowers," Steps 1–3 p. 81. Or, use large needlepoint holder with 6″ rounded piece Oasis firmly on top. Cover with German statice.

2. Make background for bouquet placing 3 longest goldenrod stems about 20″ high in center; add shorter stems deep in center covering 1st stems. Add longer stems extending out at sides, short stems near rim to fill in. Repeat, using white statice. Some statice & goldenrod should be deep in center to cover mechanics.

3. Place a slender flag-blue delphinium stem at center about 25″ high. Follow with 3 shorter stems of varying lengths in an open triangle, keeping stem ends at Main Axis, see Sketch, Spiral remaining delphinium of varying lengths to rim, using largest flowers with shortest stems near base. If florets break off, glue back using DuPont Cement.

4. Add peonies: start with smallest near top center below top delphinium. Spiral all peonies down to bowl rim. Add roses: start near top peony with lg. bud close to center; spiral down through arrangement placing some deeper, others extended from mass. Add larkspur and peony leaves: place some leaves deep in center, others out at sides near base. Place larkspur out from mass for airiness. Add bachelor buttons & echinops where space permits placing some near top, others extended at sides.

Country French flowers
See Color Photograph of p. 4.

The large sandlewood compote contains an arrangement made in the compact French style, similar to a rounded topiary. The bowl is 9" high and 9" across. A liner-bowl is used and the tight appearance of flowers is relieved by inserting green dried cattail leaves for lightness and movement. Figure: 9" ht. of bowl × 2½ = 22½" height and width of finished bouquet.

You will need:

2 Oasis bricks

Metal bowl-liner

Oasis glue, floral clay

Lg. bch. German statice

*36 clusters yellow Acacia

Lg. bch. Baby's breath

10 lg. carnation-type marigolds 3"–4" each; "Golden or Diamond Jubilee"

9 lg. parrot tulips 3"–5" each, red & white

13 or more green cattail leaves

Butterfly

Preparing the flowers:

Cut dried Acacia stems 10" long, wire & tape to # 18 wire 5" long, Step 19, p. 43. Make 36 thick clusters.

Make 12 large sprays Baby's breath.

Glue marigolds, p. 45; Calyx holding petals should be filled with DuPont cement to hold petals firm. Wire & tape to # 18 wire 12"–15" long. Steps 1–4, p. 39–40. Stand in styrofoam; spray with Petalspray 3 times, see p. 46.

Wire & tape tulips as above, using # 18 wire 10–12" long. Spray lightly.

Cut cattail leaves 8"–10" long; wire & tape using # 18 wire 5" long.

*Acacia: Trees are common in California, blooming in Jan. & Feb. Buy packaged fresh Acacia from florist, dry by immersing in Petalast or by hanging.

Putting it all together:

1. Hold Oasis bricks together, cut to fit liner-bowl. Cover liner-bowl bottom generously with Oasis glue, spreading with brush, then place Oasis bricks tightly in bowl as shown. Weight to dry. Needlepoint holder may be substituted for glue.

2. With paring knife, pare Oasis into a round ball extending above liner-bowl 2″ higher in center. Place bowl in compote with floral clay around bottom to hold firmly in place.

3. Cut pile of 1½″–2″ lengths German statice. Insert statice in Oasis, covering edge of bowl first, then work from top down to cover.

4. Begin placing Acacia, starting at top center with first stem 13" in height. Spiral Acacia clusters closely together from top to bottom, working in the round (see sketch p. 33). Bouquet should be seen from all sides and your massed flowers will now be about 20" wide and 20" high, from table. Next add Baby's breath here and there, letting it extend out from Acacia for airiness.

5. Add marigolds and tulips: Start at top of bouquet and place alternately the smallest tulip and smallest marigold. Do not be too uniform: spiral flowers extending some *out* from the mass. Cut stems shorter as needed.

6. Insert cattail leaves, using long-nose pliers. Start with 2 or 3 leaves upright near top of arrangement extending out several inches from mass. Insert other leaves horizontally into the mass, extending them out 5" or more. You may use fewer or more leaves. If cattail leaves are not available, use fern, Mahonia leaflets or other spikey leaf forms. Place butterfly.

One sided bouquets
colonial and modern

The Williamsburg Delft jar

See Color Photograph p. 8.

The container is a Williamsburg Delft jar of blues and grays. The one-sided high triangular arrangement of blues and grays, with deeper blue delphinium and bachelor buttons follows the windswept design on container. Many one-sided arrangements are placed against walls or mirrors where height is desirable; in using delphinium, it is easier to make a high arrangement due to the length of stems. Container is 8″ high; figure height: $2\frac{1}{2}-4 \times 8'' = 20''-32''$ high, 21″ wide, and 12″–15″ in depth. This arrangement is 30″ high.

You will need

Sand or buckshot

Oasis

German statice

18 delphinium stalks, light to dark blue

1 large bunch silver artemesia

15 blue echinops (globe thistle)

45 deep blue bachelor buttons

Butterfly

Preparing the flowers

Extend 5 of the most graceful stems of delphinium with # 18 wire to 24″ long, Step 22, p. 44. Extend other stems to 18″–20″ long.

Break up bunch of artemesia into 24 pieces, cutting stems into sections of 3–5 pieces (or more); tape these twice to # 18 wire, Steps 6–8, p. 40–41.

Extend stems of echinops to 18″–20″ with 2–3 thistles; follow Steps 5–8, p. 40–41.

Glue bachelor buttons on short stems, p. 45. When dry, cluster 3–5 per stem in varying lengths on # 18 wire; extend to 15″–20″, Step 16, p. 43.

Putting it all together:

1. Fill bottom 3″ of container with clean, dry sand or buckshot for weight. Fill remaining part of jar with left-over pieces of Oasis to within 2″ of top. Cut ½ block Oasis to fit into neck of jar and extend over top 2″, rounding it into muffin shape.

2. Stabilize Oasis by forcing 3 # 18 wires into jar to bottom. Cut off wire even with top. Or run ¼″ strip Davee tape over top; anchor at each side to jar rim.

3. Cut bunch German statice into 1½″–3″ pieces. Begin to cover at rim, inserting pieces all around. Insert at top center overlapping down to rim until Oasis is completely covered.

4. Place longest delphinium stalk ⅔ to rear of jar, to height of 30" or less. Follow with 3 shorter varying length stems: 1 in back of the first and tallest, then 1 to right and 1 to left of first stem, flaring them out to form triangle at top. Keep stem ends together.

5. Add silver artemesia spikes behind, in front and to each side of delphinium. Stay within a triangle about 21" wide at rim.

6. Continue adding delphinium at sides; extend 1 short stemmed, heavily flowered deep blue stem directly out near front center rim. Add 3 more lighter blue spikes on the right side. Repeat with artemesia until almost all delphinium and artemesia have been used.

7. Place blue echinops: start at top center graduating down on left side in flowing left zigzag line, balancing delphinium and artemesia and adding feeling of movement and motion (as design on jar).

8. Fill in rear of jar with left-over artemesia and 1 or 2 short delphinium stems for dimension looking thru and beyond.

9. Add bachelor buttons last. Concentrate them near center and on either side of echinops, extending out to the right side at base to emphasize windswept pattern. Glue butterfly deep in center. Spray bouquet, p. 46.

The Williamsburg bricks

See Color Photographs p. 11, and Inside Front Cover.

There are several sizes of Delft Bricks, the Williamsburg narrow blue and white brick, and a larger "Sleepy Hollow" brick (the one shown here) which is 6½" wide, 4" high and 3½" deep. Figuring the size: 2½–3 × 6½" = 15"–20" high and wide. This red, white, blue and gold fan arrangement measures 18" high and wide, meant for use on a mantel or table.

You will need

Sand or buckshot

Oasis and Davee tape

German statice

3 leatherleaf fern stems

Lg. bch. green goldenrod

15 stems white larkspur

3 doz. blue salvia stems

3 doz. yellow acroclinium

Lg. bch. acacia

15 stems Connecticut Yankee blue delphinium

3 small–med. double white tulips

15 "Gypsy" rose buds

1 doz. blue bachelor buttons

Flower Substitutions, see p. 91.

Preparing the flowers

Wire and tape fern tips (cut top and side pieces from large fronds) extended to 10"–15", Step 12, p. 42.

Wire and tape 11 green goldenrod 6" stems, extend to 10"–15", Step 19, p. 43. Make 15 6" long goldenrod-fern clusters and acacia.

Wire and tape clusters of 2–3 acroclinium, extended to 8"–10", Step 20, p. 44.

Extend short larkspur and delphinium to 6"–12"; see Steps 5–8 p. 40–41.

Wire and tape roses and tulips to 10", Step 1–4, p. 39–40. Glue, p. 45.

Glue bachelor buttons, p. 45; cluster on short natural stems, extend to 10", Step 16, p. 43.

Cluster salvia, Step 15, p. 42. Place all flowers on styrofoam; spray, p. 46.

Putting it all together:

1. Fill bottom ⅔ of brick with clean, dry sand or ½" buckshot; then stuff odd-sized left-over pieces Oasis into sides, bottom and center until brick is filled to top. (Gives a solid base for wires to mesh together.) Press Oasis on brick for impression; cut this rectangular piece about 6¼" × 3" × 1½".

2. Shave off diagonally 1" from top front of Oasis. Round off all sharp corners. Place Oasis on brick; secure with 3 6" # 18 wires run thru to bottom. Cut wire even with top. Tear off ¼" strip Davee tape 12" long; place across rear top of Oasis and down sides of brick 1"; secure with cross-piece tape near rim on sides.

3. Cut large pile of 1"–3" pieces German statice; cover Oasis on rim edge of brick all around; then cover top down until all Oasis is lightly covered.

4. Make fan-shaped background starting 1″ from back of Oasis with fern and goldenrod. Insert wires thru brick holes where possible. Fan should be 18″ at top center; graduate sides. Bend leaf wires to right or left; on sides near rim, place leaves horizontally. Place goldenrod clusters behind fern for support and in center and sides near front to form background.

5. Add larkspur and blue salvia beginning at top center, extended between fern tips to complete fan shape. Place some in center 2″ lower than fern and at each side near front. Seen from side, fan will be slightly curved forward at sides. Add acroclinium, some at top center. Fill in center and sides with yellow acacia stems, extended so they are not buried.

6. Add delphinium, a little shorter than larkspur, placing them at top, sides and deep in center. Add tulips in zigzag; start with smallest to left of center about ⅔ height of bouquet, followed with next largest to right of center, largest at center front extended 2″ over rim.

7. Add roses and bachelor buttons. Place rose bud 3″ lower than top center; follow with others in an irregular row around inside of fan, some extended at sides and largest near front center. Repeat using all bachelor buttons.

8. Examine bouquet from the sides and front; if one side appears heavier than the other, add some unused fern, acroclinium, larkspur, etc. to fill in any holes. Few sprigs acacia at center front, extended out from other flowers, avoids a flat look. Turn bouquet to back; fill in with extra leaves, goldenrod. If any wires stick out, clip them off.

Note: Place bouquet where it will be used; if above eye level, you may need to pull a few larger flowers out and bend them down to avoid a stiff appearance. Spray, p. 46.

Substitute Flowers:

For Fern Tips: Mahonia, magnolia, beech, birch, Dusty Miller or lambs ears, etc.

For Larkspur: Deutzia, spirea, delphinium, green cattail leaves, etc.

For Acroclinium: Mini strawflowers, tiny yarrow, tansy, cupid's dart, yellow immortelles, etc.

For Acacia: Yellow annual statice, baby's breath, plume celosia, etc.

For Roses: Any other rose, large strawflowers, small crested celosia, marigolds, small tulips.

For Tulips: Small single peonies, green "Envy" zinnias, carnations, etc.

For Bachelor Buttons: Forget-me-not, scabiosa, blue verbena, blue annual statice, white anemone.

Williamsburg Posey Holder
See Color Photograph, p. 14.

This Colonial fan type container is a Williamsburg reproduction and is used for one-sided arrangements. The height of the container is 8″, so figure: 2½–3 × 8″ = 20″–24″ high and wide.

You will need

Sand and Oasis

7 narrow mahonia leaves

5 pink plume celosia

15 stems deep pink larkspur

1 bch. green goldenrod

1 bch. white annual statice

1 lg. stem silver artemesia

15 pink and white miniature strawflowers

4 med. and 1 lg. rose zinnias

6 small green "Envy" zinnias

2 small–med. pink single peonies (seashell)

45 stems lily of valley + 5 leaves

Preparing the flowers

Cut mahonia leaves 8″–10″ long; wire and tape to #20 wire, extend to 18″ long, Step 13, p. 42.

Cut celosia 5″ long; wire and tape to extend to 15″, Step 23, p. 44.

Make 2 doz. goldenrod-white statice clusters 10″–15″ long, Step 19, p. 43.

Extend larkspur to 15″; see Steps 5–8, p. 40–41.

Wire and tape 1 doz. short tip ends artemesia; follow Steps 5–8, p. 40–41.

Tape strawflower stems; see Steps 1–4, p. 39–40; extend 7 stems to 12″, Step 8, p. 41.

Wire and tape peonies and zinnias, Steps 1–4, p. 39–40; glue, p. 45. Stand upright on styrofoam; spray all flowers, p. 46.

Make 15 lily of valley clusters, Step 14, p. 42; tape leaves, Step 10, p. 41. Spray with other flowers.

Alternate color and flower combinations: See p. 95.

Note: It is *extremely* difficult to get flower materials in the container without small pliers. Place and cut flower stems with pliers.

Putting it all together:

1. Weight container ⅔ full with clean, dry sand or it will be top-heavy when completed. Make 5 finger-shaped wedges dry Oasis 3″ long, trimming to fit holder. Cut level with "finger" tops.

2. Begin as far back in container as you can, placing 3 slender mahonia leaves in center finger and 1 each in others. Cut wires shorter where needed, placing them as deep as possible; bend to make them graceful. Top leaf should be 20″ high (use yardstick to measure).

3. Place celosia, 1 stem in each finger in between and a little lower than leaves to complete the fan, staying as far back as possible. There are so many wires, you must conserve space.

4. Place some larkspur stems in front of mahonia leaves letting delicate tips extend a little above mahonia. Hold some for Step 8.

5. Place 3 long goldenrod-statice clusters in center finger in front of larkspur, but shorter. Add more clusters in each finger between the leaves. Add clusters in center at about ½ the total height for background filler. Add few sprigs artemesia.

6. Place tiny strawflowers (those with longest stems) between larkspur and celosia spikes about 2"–3" shorter than leaf tips.

7. Now place smallest rose and green zinnias close to top center about 13" high and the others in a fan just below strawflowers with 2 low ones on each side. Make your flowers look up, to right or to left, but *not all facing front* like soldiers in a row!

8. Place smaller peony ⅔ up in center finger with flower looking up to the left off-center. Add the large zinnia a little lower, looking left. Now add largest peony, extended 2″ out in front—run wire through horizontally and bend into bouquet at back. A small peony bud can be added.

9. Place remaining larkspur and all lily of valley clusters in center between peonies and here and there. Add valley leaves low on each side and a few small ones deep in center. Examine bouquet to see if it is balanced. If used on mantel, place it now and adjust flowers—a falling-backward appearance can be adjusted by pulling some flowers and leaves forward and down. Spray bouquet, p. 46.

Note: If you can't get all wires into fingers, dip wire or stem end in glue and place in mass. If any wires stick out at back, snip them off, bend ends back into bouquet.

Substitutions for flowers:

For Leaves: Any preserved or glycerined leaves: beech, fern, rose, peony leaflets, small magnolia, laurel, etc.

For Peonies: Large delphinium florets, large roses, large strawflowers, zinnias, tulips, crested celosia, yarrow, etc.

For Mini Strawflowers: Small immortelle clusters, pearly everlastings, acroclinium.

For Lily of Valley: Baby's breath, squirrel-tail grass, small green cattail leaf tips, salvia, green fern or herbs.

Other Color Combinations:

Red and Gold: Use red plume celosia, white larkspur, white and red mini strawflowers, deep red and yellow zinnias and marigolds and baby's breath or blue salvia.

Yellow or Blue: Use acacia or celosia, blue delphinium for larkspur, yellow strawflowers or acroclinium, blue bachelor buttons, white small peonies, yellow zinnias, blue salvia, blue statice.

The antique glass vase

See Color Photograph p. 23.

Flowers In Antique Lamp,
a variation, page 98.

See Color Photograph p. 22.

Using crystal bowls and compotes: When you are using a low crystal compote or bowl, try to use a smaller bowl insert, see p. 36. Insert bowls should have Oasis shaved to fit with 1" or so extending above rim, rounded off and glued in place with Oasis glue. This leaves crystal exposed and all mechanics covered with flowers and leaves. After preparing bowl, follow bouquet instructions for any centerpiece in this book.

If a crystal vase has a very small opening, use the top from a spray can fitted with a small pinholder or glued-in Oasis, fastening it into the opening with clay.

This all pink, one-sided arrangement is made in a glass vase measuring 10" in height. Figure size: 2½–3 x 10" = 25"–30" high; 20"–25" wide and 15" deep at rim. Use a candle collar holder adapter.

You will need

Oasis and candle collar adapter
Oasis glue
White clay, "Cling"
Buckshot
German statice
11 slender mahonia leaves
Large bch. green goldenrod
20 pink larkspur stems
5 single pink peonies (3 small 2"–3" and 2 large 5"–6")
5 double deep pink peonies (medium to large)
8–9 pink zinnias
5 peony leaflets
13 green cattail leaves 10–13" long
6 stems baby's breath

Preparing the flowers

Wire and tape mahonia, Step 13, p. 42: Make 5 stems extended 12" long, 6 stems extended 15" long.

Wire and tape goldenrod in slender long clusters: 5 extended 20" long, 10 extended to 15" long, 12 extended to 10" long, Step 19, p. 43.

Wire and tape peonies and zinnias 12"–20" long; stand upright on styrofoam, Steps 1–4, p. 39–40, #20 wire. Glue and spray, p. 45–46.

Extend larkspur to 12"–20" long, Steps 5–8, p. 40–41.

Extend peony leaves to 12"–15", Step 11, p. 41.

Wire and tape cattail leaves, extend to 15"–20" on #20 wire, Step 12, p. 42.

Wire and tape 6" stems baby's breath using #22 wire, extend to 12"–15"; see Step 9, p. 41.

Putting it all together:

1. Make impression on Oasis with candle collar; cut to fit, extending 2″ above edge of collar. Round top and sides. Pour 1 tablesp. Oasis glue into holder, set Oasis firmly, let dry. Run white Cling around outer edge of collar, anchor it on vase top. (If using candlestick, place Cling on plug.) Cut out narrow wedge 1″ × ½″ of Oasis near rim, pour in glue, fill with buckshot. Let dry. Weight counter-balances front preventing bouquet from tipping forward.

2. Mark front of vase so buckshot is in rear. Cover top and sides of Oasis with German statice cut in 1″–3″ pieces, inserting them at collar edge first, then top and sides. Place vase directly in front of you, stand while making arrangement.

3. Place tallest mahonia leaf ⅔ back on statice to height of 29″. Add shorter leaf behind this one, then 1 leaf in front to left of center at 27″, and another right of center at 25″, forming top triangle. Place shorter leaves from mid-center to rim with a leaf extending in front 13″. Place lots of green goldenrod—longest stems at top center 28″ high, a few in back at 25″; fill in sides and center with shorter pieces.

4. Place the 3 longest larkspur stems at top near center at heights of 25″–28″, forming an open triangle. Insert stems close together at base. Add larkspur at sides and close to rim. Hold a few stems to be added later.

5. Place smallest single peony within larkspur triangle at top center. Add second single peony 4″ lower than first and a little left of center. Add smallest double peony 4″ below and a little right of center. Place another single peony high in the *back* of arrangement at 25″. Add remaining 2 large single peonies, one looking a little to right and one a little left of center near rim. Add double peonies, one at each side, bending stems to hang a bit.

6. Add zinnias: smallest one high in arrangement close to top peony, several in the *back*, and some on sides and center wherever they will fit gracefully. Peonies should form a lazy S line zig-zagging to rim with zinnias complimenting them.

7. Finish arrangement adding peony leaves in middle center and sides and one extending out in front near rim. Place cattail leaves, using some near top and sides extending out farther than flowers. Add rest of larkspur at front center; fill in with clouds of baby's breath, keeping arrangement light and airy. Cover glass with plastic wrap; spray bouquet, p. 46.

Flowers in Antique Lamp, see Color Photo p. 22.

Follow Steps 1–3 p. 97 placing floral clay around collar stem, rather than cup edge. Adapt ht. and width to size of lamp following measurement instructions p. 96. SUBSTITUTE: dried Acacia branches, wired and taped for Mahonia and goldenrod. Use tulips, roses, single peonies and leaves in zigzag line as shown, follow Steps 5–7, above.

The Country French Figurine

See Color Photograph p. 19.

The bronze figurine is a dominant accessory and a part of this high traingle arrangement. It was designed to compliment a French impressionist landscape in which blues, greens, whites and gold predominate, so these colors are used in the flowers. The bronze is 17″ high, so figure: 1½–2 x 17″ = 26″–34″ and 17″ wide. A semi-circular needlepoint holder is used to hold flowers and fits around back of figurine. This arrangement is 30″ high.

You will need

Oasis and needlepoint holder, 6″ x 2″ x 1½″ high

2–3 leatherleaf fern stems

1 lg. bch. green goldenrod

8 long stems delphinium, light to deep blue

18 stems bearded wheat

2–3 stems baby's breath

5 miniature yarrow

8–9 green "Envy" zinnias

13 anemone Japonica with stems, buds, leaves

Preparing the flowers

Wire and tape 3 10″ long stems goldenrod, extended to 24″, Step 19, p. 43. Extend 9 shorter stems to 8″, 12″, and 15″ lengths. Hold short pieces.

Cut all leaflets from fern stems; wire and tape to extend to 6″–12″, Step 12, p. 42.

Extend 3 delphinium to 27″–30″ on # 18 wire, Step 22, p. 44. Extend 5 large-flowered stems to 10″–15″.

Cut wheat stems 7″ long; tape to # 18 wire in clusters of 2–3 extended to 10″–25″, Step 19, p. 43.

Cut short lateral sprays baby's breath; tape to # 18 wire extended to 10″, 15″, 18″, Step 19, p. 43.

Cut yarrow 9″ long; insert # 18 wire into stems, Step 23, p. 44, extend to 18″–29″.

Wire and tape zinnias, extend to 10″–25″. Place upright on styrofoam; glue and spray, p. 45–46.

Wire and tape anemones in clusters 7″ long, natural stems extended to 15″–25″, Step 21 p. 44. Spray, p. 46.

Putting it all together:

1. Cut Oasis to fit holder, pressing firmly on pins. It should be 1″ higher than holder. Round top and sides. Place 7 wired fern tips at back extended one at center to 15″ high, shorter pieces on each side. Extend fern out at sides. Cover Oasis lightly with short pieces unwired goldenrod to form a triangular background.

2. Place tallest delphinium spike 30″ high in center near back of holder; follow with 2 more stems, one to left and one slightly forward to the right, forming irregular triangle. At base, stems should be *very close* together, open at top. Add remaining delphinium, one in back at 12″ high, others lower on sides, and some extended out near base at sides.

3. Add tallest plumey wired green goldenrod to fill in the triangle at top center. Add remaining irregular length wired pieces behind delphinium and on sides, forming a background for the figure.

4. Place figurine in front of holder so head is directly under the top delphinium stem. Add wheat spray near figure's head; add more wired fern and wheat, each a little lower than preceding stems, extended out at sides near base. Add baby's breath for contrast and airiness.

5. Place 1"–2" sized yarrow, smallest one high over the head of figure. Add several others at sides and near base. Add green zinnias, one high up at about 25", then zigzag these down on either side of figurine to base with largest flowers on shortest stems at sides.

6. Add anemones, smallest ones high up, others here and there within triangle, leaving them casual. Place some near skirt at base. Examine arrangement—wherever the holder is exposed, add a few pieces green goldenrod, fern, etc. Fill in back in the same way. If flowers are not completely stable, drip some Dupont's cement into the Oasis in center; let dry. Remove figure; spray flowers, p. 46.

A branch with peony

See Color Photograph p. 20.

Each modern arrangement is a separate experience and cannot be exactly duplicated. When pruning star magnolia, willows, wisterias, etc. save the interesting curved branches for future use. This container is 12″ high, so figure: 2½–3 x 12″ = 30″–36″. The arrangement is 36″ high.

You will need

A branch

1½″ ball Oasis

Dry moss

3–5 peony leaves

1 large tree peony (this is yellow, "Argosy")

Alternate flower substitutions, see p. 103.

Preparing the flowers

Wire peony leaves, extending stems to 5″–6″ in length, Step 11, p. 41. Dip wire end in glue before inserting into stem. Place upright on styrofoam.

Wire and tape peony to #22 wire stem 5″ long, Steps 1–4, p. 39–40.

Glue and spray peony and spray peony leaves 2 coats Petalspray, see p. 45 and 46.

Putting it all together:

1. Start with a beautifully hand-crafted 12″ high ceramic container of pale gray, green-gray, and delicate spattering of pale orange. Top opening is ½″, so lower part of branch was shaved to fit. To stabilize branch, insert small ball of clay at top opening.

2. Cut small ball of Oasis 1½″ in diameter; glue this with Oasis glue high up in branch, let dry. Cover ball with dried moss glued on in small pieces with Dupont's cement.

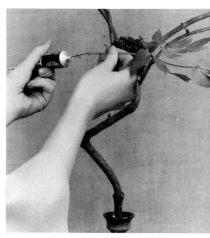

3. Dip wired leaves into tube of cement, running them through Oasis *horizontally*. Keep leaves away from branch, placing one in front extending out, two in back at different levels, and another closer to center—the effect will be of a bird in flight. Snip off exposed wire ends extending from Oasis.

4. Dip peony wire in glue, then place in center, looking up to the sky and about 2″ above the Oasis. Cut stem to fit. When glue is dry, flower will be stable.

Substitutions: Large hybrid deGraff lilies, large California giant zinnias, lily flowered tulips, or any other large flower. Use peony leaves or any interesting large leaves.

Gift from your garden

See Color Photograph p. 10

This red, white and blue arrangement of roses, peonies and delphinium with deep blue bachelor buttons in an old blue apothecary jar would be a decorative addition to many rooms. The masses of olive green goldenrod and white statice make the flowers appear freshly picked. The container and base are 6″ high and the finished one-sided arrangement becomes 30″ in height, using a formula of 5 × 6″ (ht. of container). It could be made 3 × 6″ in height, using fewer flowers.

You will need:

Oasis brick plus sand or buckshot

Lg. bch. German statice

40 clusters green goldenrod

1 lg. bch. white annual statice

12 stems light to med. blue delphinium Pacific Hybrids, "Bluebird" and "Blue Jay".

6–7 large white single peonies, varying sizes.

13 large red roses, bud to fully open "Tropicana" or other variety.

10 clusters bachelor buttons (about 50 flowers).

Preparing the flowers:

Wire goldenrod clusters 15″–25″ long, on # 18 wire; Step 19, p. 43.

Insert # 18 wire in delphinium stems to lengthen to 15″–25″, see Step 22, p. 44. Stand upright in styrofoam.

Tape peonies to # 18 wire 14″–18″ long.

Wire and tape roses, see Steps 1–4 p. 39–40 using # 18 wire; make stems 14″–24″ long, stand upright.

Glue bachelor button, see p. 44, Make clusters using 5 irregular length stems 4″–6″ long on # 18 wire; see Step 16, p. 43.

Spray all flowers 2 coats Petalspray, see Spraying p. 46.

Putting it all together:

1. Fill bottom 2″ of container with dry sand or ½ lb. buckshot for weight, then fill with oasis held vertically, rounding off top about 1″ higher than rim. If any space is unfilled, shove in small leftover oasis pieces. Cover top of oasis with small pieces of German statice as shown.

2. Read "Guideposts and Guidelines" p. 30–32. Insert all the green goldenrod clusters, starting with topmost piece about 25″ high (from base) extending out at sides to about 18″ wide. After placing tall pieces, fill in center with many shorter clusters so you will have a densely filled triangular appearance. Place white annual statice in stems of varying lengths here and there.

3. Add Delphinium: Start with 3 slender blue stems, one spike in center about 30″ high, then one stem 25″ long to left and one stem 23″ long, slightly forward to right, forming a triangle. Place all stems deep in oasis to bottom of container if possible. Now place two stems one to right and left near container-rim to form sides of triangle. Fill in sides and center, adding 1 stem in back for depth.

4. Place white peonies: the longest stem and smallest flower at top center 6″ lower than top delphinium. The next largest flower is 5″ lower, leaning slightly to right, then another flower left of mid-center, and the largest open flower near base, slightly to right—giving continuous flow of white through center of arrangement. Place peony to left side as shown; then 1 or 2 near back of arrangement for depth.

5. Add roses with 1 tall bud near top center, zigzaging flowers from top to base. Place 2 buds, one at each side, bending stems downward to give natural line to triangle sides. Add all remaining roses at sides and near center as shown.

6. Lastly, add clusters of bachelor buttons, some in top center of triangle, some at sides and others running near the peonies from top to rim, permitting them to extend outward from the mass for lightness (do not bury them). Place plastic kitchen wrap on container for protection, spray entire bouquet with Petalspray.

The dolphin candlesticks

See Color Photograph p. 7.

The reproduction Sandwich Glass Dolphin candlesticks are lovely when used for bouquet holders. Other candlesticks or old lamp bases (see the Antique Glass Vase, variation p. 23) may also be used. These bouquets were made one-sided to be used on mantel or buffet but are equally attractive made in-the-round for table centerpieces. The candlesticks are 9″ high. Figure: 2½ to 3 x 9″ = 22″ to 27″ at highest and widest points, including candlestick. Adjust height and width depending on height of your candlesticks.

For each candlestick
You will need:

1 9″ candlestick
1 pewter candlestick adapter
Oasis and Oasis glue
White floral clay
½ bch. German statice
Lg. bch. green goldenrod
2 preserved Leatherleaf ferns
8 clusters short stemmed purple statice
13–15 light & dark single delphinium stems (Conn. Yankees)
4 pink single peonies, 1 bud
9 white roses (2 buds)
27 pink Anemone Japonica
½ bch. Baby's Breath
Lg. butterfly (optional)

Preparing the flowers:

Wire and tape 16 clusters green goldenrod, on # 18 wire 9″–12″ long, see Step 19, p. 43.

Cut fern fronds from stems into 6 or more. Wire and tape each as goldenrod; making them 5″–9″ long.

Wire and tape 8 short clusters purple statice to 8″ length.

Insert # 20 wire into delphinium stems, see Step 22, p. 44. Top stem should be 17″ long; others 10″–15″ long.

Wire Peonies on # 18 wire as in Step 1–3, p. 39. Make stems 9″ long for smallest, others should be 5″–7″ long.

Roses: Repeat as for peonies making stems 1½″ longer; make buds longest.

Anemones: Cluster 3 flowers per stem see Step 21, p. 41. Stems should be 5″ long with 5″ wires (10″ long).

Babys Breath: Wire and tape 13 short clusters or insert sprays into oasis.

Alternate Flowers and Centerpiece, p. 110

Putting it all together:

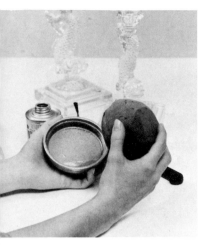

1. Press candle adapter to Oasis for impression, then cut out rounded-top ball about 3" thick at center to fit adapter. Pour about a tbsp. Oasis glue into adapter, spread over bottom and sides. Place Oasis ball in adapter; press firm, let dry.

2. Place small strip white floral clay around candle insert of adapter; place firmly in candlestick. Cover Oasis with small pieces of German statice, see Step 2, p. 97.

3. Place goldenrod spray at center point about ⅔ back from front of Oasis ball to ht. of 10" (from adapter). Behind and in front place 2 more shorter sprays. Place more sprays on each side extending out to form an 18" wide triangle. Fill in with remaining goldenrod. Place fern tips halfway up, placing one in back, several here and there near center. Extend two at sides beyond goldenrod. Place purple statice deep in center, in back and close to sides.

4. Place longest delphinium at top center. Add shorter stems behind center stem; spiral several across back and forth in front of bouquet. Add short stems at sides extending out. Add 2 longer stems, one at each side bent down. Hold remaining stems to add after peonies.

5. Add smallest peony 5" lower than top stems. Follow with larger one to left or right 5" below first, then largest peony near center base facing downward. Place one 9" long peony in rear of bouquet. Add all remaining delphinium.

6. Add rosebud near top, then another bud to rear but 3" shorter; zigzag roses left-to-right across center. Place a large rose on each side in front, bent downward.

7. Place Anemone clusters near top center and between roses and peonies extending *out* from other flowers for airiness.

8. Place Baby's Breath here and there wherever space permits. Place candlestick on mantel—you may need to lower some flowers for a better view by bending wired stems down with long nose pliers. Add extra goldenrod if needed. Glue on butterfly.

Centerpiece Round Bouquet:

When making bouquet for table use, set first goldenrod and delphinium stems in *center* of Oasis ball. Then spiral (see p. 32–33) flowers from top to bottom following above steps. Use two or three additional peonies and roses.

Alternate Flowers: Use larkspur, Acacia, plume celosia, or dried basil flowers for delphinium. Use large zinnias, crested celosia, carnations, tulips or marigolds for peonies. Substitute miniature to medium sized strawflowers or daisy-like acroclinium for roses.

"Springtime"
a natural wood sculpture
See Color Photograph p. 21

This old weathered section of burled apple tree wood was found in an orchard. It has beautiful natural lines when placed upright, with the appearance of a windswept sculpture. Nothing was done except to clean it and insert a metal rod to fit into a square wood base which takes time and patience. Since each piece of weathered or driftwood will have different dimensions, you must adjust to each. This sculpture is 27" in ht.

You will need
Weathered wood and base, see Preparation Step 1
¼" thick round metal rod about 7" long
7" square black wood base 2" thick
Small piece Oasis
Oasis glue and DuPont cement
5 plus (extras for choice) pussywillow stems freshly cut about 10"–18" long
5 pipe cleaners or twistems
3–4 stems 5" long, silver poplar leaves, galax or other pressed leaves on short stems
3 large Daffodils, single or double and 1 daffodil bud on 6" stem
5–7 daffodil leaves about 7"–9" long
18 and # 20 floral wire and olive green floratape

Advance preparation of wood & pussywillows:
One week or more before making arrangement:

1. Drill 3″–4″ long hole in base of burlwood with ¼″ drill bit. Fit a 7″ long metal rod into hole, leaving 3″–4″ of the rod extending out. Black wood base is 7″ square, 2″ thick and heavy enough to support sculpture. Drill hole in top center of base, insert metal rod holding sculpture upright.

2. Remove sculpture, place vertically on table. Glue rounded piece of Oasis 2″ x 3″ inside wood with Oasis glue applied generously on bottom. Cover with a weight; let dry. Place upright again.

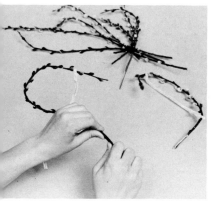

3. Cut fresh pussywillow branches. Bend lower half of varying length stems by pressing down firmly with thumbs and fingers, bending until stem yields but does not break. Move up to opposite end and continue to bend down so stem assumes a half circle curve. Tie stem tip ends lightly with pipecleaners or twistems as shown. Let dry out for a week to hold shape; remove twistems.

Putting it all together:

4. Shorten 3 pussywillow branches for best length and lines (try different lengths before cutting). Sharpen stem ends into slender points, dip in Dupont cement and place, one at a time, in Oasis on right side extending out and down, curving back toward center of wood. Let dry. Two top branches should soar out, then curve in toward center. Glue in place and let dry.

5. Wire and tape poplar, or other leaves to #20 wire cut 2" long. Wire and tape daffodils, bud stem, and daffodil leaves—see Steps 1-4 p. 39-40 and Step 10 p. 41 using #20 wire cut 4-5" long. Insert poplar leaves into Oasis first dipping ends in DuPont cement. (Leaves cover mechanics and add texture).

6. Place daffodil bud near lower right pussywillow stem; glue in place. Add open flower in center extended out 3" or more; glue in place. Add 3rd flower at upper left facing up and extending out from wood. Glue spikey daffodil leaves, shortened if needed, in place around daffodils. Squirt a little DuPont Cement into center of Oasis to stabilize all stems.

Alternate Flowers and Leaves: Use single or double tulips, large anemones, azalea blossoms or any other spring flower for daffodils. Use galax, dried cattail leaf tips, glycerined mahonia tips, azalea or Pieris Japonica for leaves.

Peonies and pussywillows
See Color Photograph p. 9

This classic arrangement of pussywillows, Japanese peonies and peony leaves takes patience, preparation and time. Ideally, all the branches should be prepared in early spring, then stored until fall. Peonies and leaves should be preserved, then stored in security boxes for the summer. Plan to prepare the branches early in spring when the sap has made them very pliable but catkins are not fully developed. Bend branches soon after cutting; do not place in water.

The ginger jar and rosewood base together total 9″ in ht. The jar is prepared so stems are arranged on an elevated base within the jar for easier insertion. The pussywillows are arranged in "Heaven," "Man" and "Earth" lines, with the "Heaven" group soaring to 27″ at the highest point when measured from top of jar.

Figure: 3 (or more) x 9″ (jar-base ht.) = 27″ or higher. This arrangement is 36″ at highest point measured from table (27″ plus 9″). A smaller jar would be scaled down using 2½ to 3 x ht. of jar for overall height of arrangement.

You will need:
20 freshly cut pussywillow branches measuring 15″ to 30″ in length
Ginger Jar with base
6″ high columnar candle 2″ thick
Paraffin for melting (use old candle ends) & Pyrex cup or can for melting (set cup in hot water)
2 Needlepoint holders
    1 lg. heavy one to hold prepared branches
    2″ wide holder for jar-top
Oasis
5 pink or white Japanese peonies, large bud to open flowers
12–13 Japanese or tree peony leaves
DuPont Cement

Preparing pussywillows & container:

1. Cut fresh pussywillow branches; have heavy needlepoint holder nearby. Follow photo and sketch, right. Bend longest delicate stem pressing down firmly at bottom third with thumbs and fingers until it yields; reverse stem, move up ⅓ length and repeat to form lazy S curve. Repeat procedure so stem holds curve. Place on holder, tie small metal weight near tip end for a day to bend tip downward.

Bend all other stems in "Heaven" group in shorter lazy S curves with tips pointing up. Bend 3 shorter stems for "Man" group in soft curves. Bend 3 "Earth" stems to a gentle semi circle with tips up. Bend all remaining stems; place on holder and let dry a week. Store until needed.

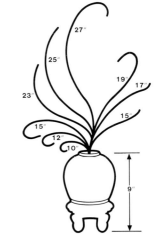

2. *Prepare Ginger Jar:* Shorten 2″ thick columnar candle to fit 2″ below rim of jar. Pour melted paraffin ½″ deep into jar, place candle upright in wax, let set. Pour hot wax on candle top, press 2″ wide needlepoint holder on top; let set. Cut Oasis to fit jar rim, press down firmly into needlepoint, cut off even with jar top.

When Ready to Make Arrangement: Glue backs of peonies, see p. 45. Wire and tape peonies and leaves to # 18 wire, using olive tape, see Step 1–4, p. 39–40 making bud stem 20″ long, remaining stems 15″, 11″, 7″ and 5″ long. Place in styrofoam. Tape smallest leaves 18″ long, 2 larger ones 13″ long, 5 leaves 10″ long, see Steps 5–8 p. 40–41. All others may be 3″–5″ long. Lightly spray, see p. 46.

Putting it all together:

3. All stems should radiate from central point on holder. Cut stem ends diagonally and firmly place 3 "Heaven" stems starting with 27" long stem at center slightly back toward rear of jar with tip hanging directly over center of jar. Place 25" stem against and forward of first stem; 23" stem against and forward of second stem.

Place "Man" group forward but very close to "Heaven" group facing right, with tallest stem 19" then next 17" and 3rd stem 15" long. Place "Earth" group close to "Man" but to left. Place stems upright, then gently pull downward to desired position. They should reach out to left, then curve back toward center. Place few shorter stems in back of arrangement for depth, and a few in front of "Man" group.

4. Add longest peony bud *behind* top pussywillow stems looking up and left. Add next smallest peony 5" lower and to right of first, between "Heaven" and "Man" groups facing right. Place large peony at left center face up. Add largest peony on 5" long stem close to base and near center with top-most pussywillow tip hanging directly over it. Add 7" long peony behind "Man" group facing rearward.

5. Add Leaves: place most delicate leaves near top bud in front and back of groups. Add shorter leaves in back and near front of rim in large cluster reaching outward to balance "Man" group. Leaves cover Oasis. When everything is in place, carefully pour DuPont cement into Oasis to fill holes and anchor stems.

116

For brides only
Sentiment
and nostalgia

Nosegays

See Color Photograph p. 12–13

Ideal for shower gifts to bridesmaids or for mothers to carry, these dainty nosegays can be made in advance and arranged for a bridal shower centerpiece or whatever.

The 3 combinations shown in color photograph, p. 12–13 are made in these combinations:

Rose and Deep Blue: Deep pink rosebud, 6–7 baby's breath clusters, white statice, 6–7 white acroclinium, 7 leatherleaf fern tips, 7 blue bachelor buttons and gold velvet ribbon ¼" wide.

Pink and Yellow: Apricot pink rosebud, 7 yellow acroclinium, 6 clusters baby's breath, 7 clusters light blue statice, 6 clusters small yellow immortelles, and pink velvet ribbon ¼" wide.

Pink and Mauve: Deep pink rosebud, 7 small white acroclinium, 6 clusters baby's breath, 5 clusters blue statice (or purple), 6 mauve pink globe amaranths, moss green velvet ribbon ¼" wide.

You will need

Corsage type #24 or #28 wire

Olive green floratape

4½" lace paper or plastic nosegay holders

¼" velvet ribbon

Selection of flowers (above)

Leatherleaf fern tips

Preparing the flowers

Wire all flowers to 5" wire stem taped to end.

Rosebud: wire, tape, Steps 1–4, p. 39–40. Glue, p. 45; Spray 2 coats, p. 46.

Bachelor buttons: run wire thru short stem (1") into calyx; tape to end. Glue, p. 45.

Glue backs of acroclinium at stem; wire and tape, Steps 1–4, p. 39–40. If they come off, glue back on.

Make 2" clusters baby's breath.

Putting it all together:

1. Hold rosebud in your left hand and tape a few sprigs baby's breath and statice around it. *Do not detach tape.*

2. Surround rose with acroclinium: tape 1–2 to rose stem at a time, making them ½″ shorter. Continue until all are taped in place; add a few more sprigs baby's breath and white statice (can be glued in later if it comes off).

3. Tape row of bachelor buttons or globe amaranths or immortelles, making these shorter than preceding flowers. Each circle of flowers should be as perfect as possible—each is wider than the one before it, each is set back farther behind the rosebud. Finished bouquet extends out at center 2½″ from flowers in last row.

4. Tape on 5 leaf tips. Tear tape off. Tape all stems together into *one smooth stem*, starting just under the last row; tape to end of stems.

5. Slip through nosegay holder (snip to open wider if needed). If there are any holes in nosegay, glue in a few florets of statice or an extra flower or fern tip. Make small bow with 5″ streamers, twist at center with short piece wire, then tape wire to nosegay stem.

A bride's bouquet

See Color Photograph p. 12.

Made in an old Milk Glass Smoke Bell, these pretty bells were used in the 19th century to protect the ceiling from smoke—thus the name, "smoke bell". They are ruffled or crimped and vary in size from 5"-7".

You will need

Oasis, 1" pinholder, Cling
White statice
Floratape (white or green)
1 doz. peach 1"-2" rosebuds
Leatherleaf fern tips
33 lily of valley stems; 7 small leaves
12 small and 13 1½" delphinium florets on 1" stems
7 small and 18 larger clusters yellow immortelles
1 doz. small baby's breath clusters
15 1" yellow acroclinium

Preparing the flowers

Wire and tape rosebuds with fern tips, Steps 1-4, to #22 wire 5" long; p. 39-40. Glue and spray; see p. 45-46.

Wire and tape 1" delphinium stems, Steps 1-4, to 5" long, p. 39-40 Glue, Spray, p. 45-46.

Break up tiny clusters immortelles with 1" stem; wire and tape to 5" wire, Steps 6-8, p. 40-41.

Break off acroclinium stem to 2"; wire and tape each to 5" long, Step 20, p. 44. (Glue back of flowers.)

Wire and tape 1 doz. 2" clusters baby's breath on 5" wire.

Wire and tape lily of valley and leaves; cluster 3 stems 3"-5" long on 5" wire, Step 14, p. 42.

Tape leaves, Step 10, p. 41.

Putting it all together:

Note: All wire "stems" may be too long, cut to fit. Use a *long nosed pliers* to place flowers and cut stems.

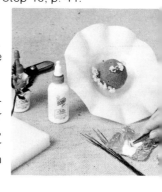

1. Place Cling around bottom edge of 1" needlepoint holder; press firmly into center of bell to anchor it. Cut a 2½" ball of Oasis, leave flat on bottom, rounding sides and top. Press onto pin holder. Cover Oasis lightly with white statice florets dipped first in Sobo glue.

2. Place most perfect rosebud in *exact center* of Oasis, extended out about 4½". Surround with 3 lily of valley clusters. Now the boquet becomes a series of *ever-widening flower circles,* each a little shorter and wider than the preceding one and flowers in outer circles become a little larger.

3. Add ring of small delphinium florets around rose, but 1" shorter-stemmed. Squeeze wire stems together gently after placing them to hold in tighter bunch. Fill in any spaces with partial row of small immortelle and baby's breath clusters.

4. Add 5 clusters of lily of valley, letting these extend out about 2" beyond other flowers to break up the pincushion look.

5. Place large rosebuds in tight, uniform circle shorter than first delphinium florets. Add larger immortelles alternately with acroclinium and large delphinium florets, filling ruffles of bell in widening circle. Add lily of valley sprays, leaves and baby's breath *almost horizontally* to stand out from bouquet about 2"-3".

6. Spray flowers lightly with Petalspray. If bouquet is made a week in advance, keep in warm, dry place or in airtight box with 2 lb. Petalast; seal tight.

Final touch: Knot white satin 36" streamers at intervals. Gather streamers together at center with fine piece wire first taped with white floratape; insert in bottom of bouquet. Make hand-hold loop of strong ribbon thru bell loop.

A bridal keepsake

The Bride's Flowers Under Glass, see Photograph p. 13.

As soon after the wedding as possible, remove all flowers and leaves from the bouquet and preserve them following directions in *"The Step-By-Step Book of PRESERVED FLOWERS"*. Usually flowers and leaves can be preserved in one box in 5–6 days. Preserve tiny ivy, smilax and other leaves and baby's breath. Use flowers from cake top-knot too. Place ribbon and tulle puffs in clean plastic bag until you are ready to make the keepsake.

When all flowers are dried, hold them in an airtight security box until heat is on and humidity is low. I prefer domes in 3 sizes: 5" x 5" high, 5" x 7" high, and 6" x 7" high, depending on size and number of flowers to be used. Higher domes can have trapped air forming an unsightly "clouding".

A Gift of Flowers Under Glass:

These make lovely and unusual gifts, especially if you select your flower colors and varieties with the recipient in mind. For someone who loves blue, use delicate sprays and florets of hybrid delphinium, bachelor buttons, lily of valley, white rosebuds and baby's breath. For other choices, use Lenten or Christmas roses (helleborous), small hybrid lilies, favorite name varieties of roses, with sprays of caryopteris, deutzia, forget-me-not, Japanese anemones (windflowers) and countless others. Tiny daffodils and other small spring bulb flowers would be beautiful choices, too. Follow Steps 1–5, p. 39–40, using preserved flowers.

You will need

Dome with wood base
Oasis glue, Sobo and silicone glue
White statice florets
While or olive floratape
¼" wide moss green velvet ribbon

Preparing the flowers

Carefully glue, wire and tape all flowers on # 24 or # 22 wire; Steps 1–4, p. 39–40 and Glueing, p. 45. Spray all flowers, p. 46.

Putting it all together:

1. Cut a circle of Oasis 1½" x 1½", tapering top and sides. Brush bottom generously with Oasis glue, then press on center of wood base. Let dry.

2. Make pile of white statice florets, then using tweezers, dip ends into puddle of Sobo glue and cover Oasis. Surround with small leaves in uniform circle. (Leaves can be cut smaller). If available, tulle puffs can be spiraled on Oasis.

3. Place smallest, delicate flowers near top center measuring stem length against dome; dip wire tips in Sobo glue and place in Oasis. Follow with larger flowers, leaves, etc. Dome pictured uses acacia, baby's breath, lily of valley and roses. Keep flowers different lengths, some glued directly to base. Cover open spots with leaves, ribbon loops, etc. Glue in butterfly.

4. Place completed arrangement (minus glass) in airtight container or in unused oven with 2 lbs. Petal-ast to dry-out for 24–48 hrs. Set wood base on foil as it should not be in direct contact with Petalast. When ready to complete the dome, polish glass with lint-free cloth or clean tissue.

5. Hold base upside down, tapping vigorously with fingertips on bottom to remove loose petals, blowing gently. Brush off crystals with artist's brush. Run silicone glue inside the "channel" in base. Gently lower glass over flowers into glue; move glass around so glue is in contact. Cut velvet ribbon to fit glass; cover lightly with Sobo, then glue around bottom of glass. Wipe off any glue with damp cloth; polish.

Things to remember:

Moist air trapped inside the dome will eventually form an unsightly "clouding" on the inside of the glass. To avoid this, cover the dried finished base arrangement of flowers (Step 4) with the clean dry dome as quickly as possible. Do so only when surrounding air is very dry, preferably when the furnace is turned on.

Domes exposed to extremes of temperature, hot or cold, may have the wood base contract, causing the glass to crack. Avoid this by sealing the dome in place with silicone glue, which seems to have a slight "give" permitting some wood contraction.

Do not display domes in direct sunlight: flowers will discolor and fade, and a possible heat build-up inside the dome can cause clouding and a film of moisture.

In tropical climates, it may be preferable to place the dome over the flowers without glueing, permitting you to clean it from time to time, though flowers may not last as well.

A wedding memory in a shadowbox

See Color Photograph p. 13.

Nothing is quite as sentimental to a bride or her mother as a few flowers from her bouquet preserved with the invitation. I have seen a few examples made before we had modern drying methods where the flowers were so brown and curled they could not be identified, but the bride, celebrating a half-century of marriage, would not part with them. Modern brides frequently plan ahead with their florists so a small nosegay is attached to the bouquet for the throwing-ceremony; *as soon after the wedding as possible,* the bouquet is taken apart for preserving flowers and leaves.

You will need

Gold shadowbox frame (these are 10″ x 12″ x 1½″)

Candlelight satin

Heavy pictureboard for backing and 4 side strips cut to fit frame sides

1½″ candlelight velvet ribbon (about 1⅓ yds)

Sobo glue

Tweezers for handling flowers

2 lbs. Petalast (for 2nd dry-out)

Aluminum foil or glass for final backing

Waterproof tape or "Contact"

Preparation

Glue glass into frame with Sobo; weight it until dry.

Cut square of satin 13″ x 15″; place under pictureboard; fold over each side and glue to board, squaring off corners neatly.

Picture side strips should be slightly shorter than frame sides for ribbon overlap. Cut ribbon 1″ wider; glue strip to ribbon flush with edge. Fold over ends; glue in place. Glue these strips, one by one, into place in frame. Glue ribbon edge near top flush with frame. Set aside.

Remove flowers from security box: Glue and spray rosebuds, bachelor buttons, etc. Use spray LIGHTLY. Let dry. See Glueing and Spraying, p. 45–46.

Putting it all together:

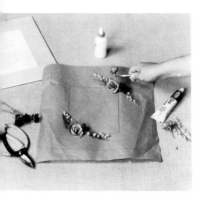

1. Take piece of wrapping paper and outline picture board with pencil. Place invitation in center where you wish it, outline this also. Glue invitation on satin-covered backing, set aside. Using paper-outline, arrange preserved flowers and leaves in a crescent design or in two L shaped nosegay clusters.

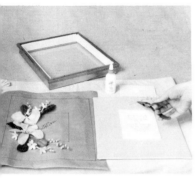

2. Examples shown are made with: Crescent-phaleanopsis orchids, stephanotis, leaves and lily of valley. L-Shape: rosebuds, bachelor buttons, lily of valley and leaves "tied" together with ¼" rose velvet ribbon.

3. Begin to remove flowers at farthest ends from middle, working in to center flowers. Use tweezers to lift flowers, dip in "puddle" of Sobo, and place in same position on satin back. Follow with leaves and larger flowers until all flower material is transferred to satin. Some leaves or flowers may overlap invitation. Add additional leaflets, etc. to fill in space. If you drop a bit of glue, cover with lily bell, small butterfly, leaflet, etc.

4. Place finished dry picture on piece of foil; place in a box with 2 lbs. Petalast on bottom and cover tightly to dry-out for 24–48 hrs. (All moisture must be removed before sealing.)

5. Carefully clean both sides of glass in frame using lint-free handiwipes or clean tissue paper. Hold flower picture upside down and tap it to remove any loose particles; brust off any crystals adhering to satin with artist's brush. Place in frame.

6. Where humid conditions are severe, glue a thin sheet of glass to back (this can be done after fabric is glued on) or glue sheet of heavy-duty aluminum foil over picture-board to edge of frame (this acts as moisture-barrier). When dry, trim off edges. Cover back with water-proof tape or "Contact" cut to fit. Fasten screw eyes and wire to frame.

A Victorian shadowbox of flowers
A Variation

Dainty floral pictures were an art form in Victorian times and are once again finding favor in today's homes. Follow "A Wedding Memory in a Shadowbox" p. 125–126. Substitute a triangular design of preserved flowers, buds, ferns, leaflets, etc. in Step 1. Outline on paper with 9 wild green tansy ferntips or other ferns; fill spaces between fern with rose leaflets, green Queen Ann's lace buds. Add short stems of Deutzia or lily of valley. Place rose leaves in center, top with medium rose in mid-center and large open rose near base. Fill in with delphinium florets, buds, leaflets. Place sprays of forget-me-not on sides and top.

Transfer design, using tweezers, starting with ferns and outline flowers. Work toward center, dipping in Sobo then in place on satin or velvet background. Cut short stems and glue just below large rose. Glue on velvet bow. Finish as in Steps 4–6.

Small things for gifts

A Pewter Salt Shaker (for a kitchen shower)

A Demi-Tasse Cup

Seeing Double — A Small Pair

A Nosegay

A Small Round Centerpiece

A Bride's Keepsake, Flowers Under Glass

A Spring Basket of Flowers

A Small Delft Arrangement

A pewter salt shaker

See Color Photograph p. 15.

A pair of these would make a welcome shower or new-house gift, especially for an early American kitchen. The salt is 3″ high so figure: 3 x 3″ = 9″ high and 7″ in the round.

You will need

Oasis
German statice
Green goldenrod
10 small orange plume celosia
1 doz. 3″ pieces gold or green decorative grass or quaking oats, etc.
7 small French marigolds
2 doz. ¼″ poppy pods
Leaflets or fern tips
Butterfly

Preparing the flowers

Break stems of celosia to 1″; extend to 4″ on # 22 wire, Step 23, p. 44
Wire and tape marigolds to 8″ length, Steps 1–4, p. 39–40.
Glue and Spray, p. 45 and 46.
Wire and tape short grasses and fern tips to 2″ wire, Step 12, p. 42.
Make 3″ long clusters poppy pods, extend to 6–7″; see Step 18, p. 43.

Substitution colors and flowers, p. 130.

Putting it all together:

1. Cut 2″ x 3½″ piece Oasis to fit inside salt shaker; center shaft holds it secure. Cut small pile German statice 1″–2″; insert around rim of salt, then on top and sides to cover Oasis.

2. Insert short 4″ stems green goldenrod in center, spiraling more pieces until you have delicate background. Insert celosia near top at 8″; spiral remaining celosia to rim. Follow with grass, oats, etc. filling in, but leave them extended out.

3. Add the smallest marigold at 8" high in center, then spiral remaining marigolds down to rim, extending out from the mass. Don't bury them.

4. Add poppy clusters with the smallest at top center 9" in height, then others spiraling between the marigolds. Fill in any spaces with goldenrod, fern tips or small leaves. Glue on butterfly. Spray bouquet with Petalspray, p. 46.

Substitution colors and flowers: Here are a few selections to choose from:

Red-White-Blue	Yellow-Blue	Blue-Green
Red plume celosia	Goldenrod	Squirrel tail grass
White statice	Yellow statice	Other green grass or herbs
White larkspur tips	Acacia sprays	
Red rosebuds	Marigolds yellow	Blue statice
Dyed red immortelles	Yellow mini strawflowers	Green helleborous
Conn. Yankee delphinium ·	Immortelle clusters	Tiny green zinnias
Blue salvia	Conn. Yankee delphinium	Off-white strawflowers
Bachelor buttons	Blue salvia	Delphinium tips
White acroclinium	Bachelor buttons	Bachelor buttons
Mini white strawflowers	Yellow acroclinium	White larkspur
		Blue floral butts

A demi-tasse cup

See Color Photograph p. 15.

The 3" cup is deep pink and arrangement is pink and white, measuring
2½–3 x 3" = 7½"–9" high and in the round.

You will need

Oasis

German statice

6 pink larkspur tips

5 leatherleaf fern tips

6 pink rosebuds

7 small goldenrod stems or acacia leaves

3 mini carnations

8 stems anemone Japonica with buds and leaves

9 lily of valley stems

Butterfly

Substitute flowers and colors, p. 132.

Preparing the flowers

Extend larkspur tips to 10" on #24 wire, Steps 6–8 p. 40–41.

Wire and tape rosebuds 5"–8" long, Steps 1–4, p. 39–40; Glue and spray, p. 45–46.

Repeat with carnations; see Glueing, p. 45.

Tape short goldenrod or acacia leaves, Step 19, p. 43.

Wire fern tips to 2" wire, Step 12, p. 42.

Wire and tape anemones to 8", Step 21, p. 44.

Make 3 lily of valley clusters 6" long, Step 14, p. 42.

Putting it all together:

1. Place 2 small pieces clay on bottom of cup; press cup to saucer so they can't separate. Cut Oasis 2½" square x 4" high, round sides, press into cup. Round off top 1" above rim. Cut 1"–2" pieces statice and insert at cup rim, then insert at top and cover Oasis completely.

2. Place 3 stems larkspur at center of Oasis, extending out in wide triangle 7″, 8″, 9″ high. Place few fern leaves in center repeating triangle.

3. Place several rosebuds high up between larkspur. Place largest rose deep in center 6″ high (like a little jewel). Surround with acacia or rose leaves or goldenrod. Add more rosebuds around center rose. (Roses are "Gene Boerner".) Keep flowers loose and airy, looking up or to left or right. Add carnations.

4. Add anemones and lily of valley clusters within triangle around rose, extending out of mass. Add few more leaflets (dip in glue). Glue on butterfly.

Substitutions: Many color combinations and substitute flowers could go into this type informal small gift. Here are a few:

For Larkspur:
Conn. Yankee delphinium tips
Heather
White or blue salvia
Tiny plume celosia tips

For Rosebuds:
Miniature strawflowers
White or yellow acroclinium
Tiny daffodils
Scabiosa
Tiny zinnias

For Carnations:
Tiny marigolds
Immortelle clusters
Statice sinuata

For Anemone Japonica:
Daisies (marguerites)
Bachelor buttons

For Lily of Valley:
Forget me not
Blue salvia
Baby's breath

Seeing double: A small pair

See Color Photograph p. 16.

These delicate, but simple, blue and white matching bouquets were made for a dresser, desk or small end tables. The vases are 5″ high, so figure: 5″ x 2½ = 12″ at highest point on completed bouquets and about 10″ wide at widest point. These were made one-sided, but could easily be viewed in-the-round.

You will need for two:
2 vases

Some clean dry sand or buckshot (for weight)

Oasis

22 floral wire and olive green floraltape

18 Blue Salvia clusters: 27 small stems 5″ long

14 white Anemone Japonica (windflowers) on stems with buds and leaves

10 Anemone leaves 2″ size

20 Forget-Me-Not stems, 4–5″ long

Preparing the flowers:
Wire & tape Salvia clusters, 3 stems on each 5″ wire, see Step 15, p. 42.

Wire & tape Anemone stems and Forget-Me-Not stems on 3″ wires, see Step 21, p. 44

Alternate flowers:

For Salvia, use: short larkspur or small delphinium stem ends; blue or white annual statice; tip ends of artemesia. For Anemones: use miniature straw-flowers, globe amaranths, small roses, acroclinium (everlasting daisies), feverfew, etc. For Forget-Me-Not: tiny fern sprays, baby's breath, dried grasses, tiny plume celosia tips, dried basil flowers.

Putting it all together:

1. Weight vases by filling bottoms 2" deep with clean sand. (Or use a tablespoonful of buckshot).

2. With paring knife, make 2 thick finger-shaped pieces of Oasis about 5" long; press into vase, cut off Oasis at top flush with rim. If wider vases are used, make Oasis wider to conform to openings.

3. Place delicate cluster blue salvia in center of vase to height of 12". Add more salvia clusters on each side of first stem, but shorter to form triangle. Add salvia to left, right and cluster in rear of vase extended outward 3" on all sides.

4. Add Anemones: place smallest flower about ⅔ up in center of salvia triangle. Place flowers, each shorter and extended out from center, looking up, by inserting wire upright with pliers, then bend down so flower is less erect. Add larger leaves near rim of vase to cover mechanics. Place forget-me-nots where space permits. Examine vases side by side; they should be reasonably similar in height and width.

Putting your bouquet away for the summer

Dried flowers, whether they are preserved in *Petalast* or dried by hanging, will suffer from humidity with mild to extreme color loss when windows are open in humid weather. Air conditioning will prevent fading, but most people prefer to alternate periods of use in their air conditioning, opening windows when it is cool and moist air enters the house to damage bouquets.

If you want to keep your bouquets for fall use, put them away for the summer. This will take good timing, as it must be done *before the heat is turned off* in the spring.

Place bouquet on a square of cardboard slightly larger than bouquet. Secure to the cardboard with 1½″ wide strips of masking tape, overlapping strips on base of flower container. Place bouquet carefully in a cardboard box large enough to avoid damaging the flowers.

Pour 3 lbs. of *Petalast* carefully around the bouquet. Cover the box, tape closed. Lift box into heavy-duty plastic bag; tape closed to make it airtight. Store in dry place.

In the fall, after the heat goes on, remove bouquet from storage. Update with some new clusters of green goldenrod and leaves; replace any faded or damaged flowers and spray lightly with Petalspray, see p. 46.

Send for the free Newsletters and Price List of flowers, cones, pods, mechanical aids, and the flower preservatives: Petalast and Petalspray. **Please enclose stamp.**

ROBERTA MOFFITT P.O. BOX 3597, WILMINGTON, DEL. 19807